*Birth & Rebirth*
*on an Alaskan Island*

# Birth & Rebirth
## on an Alaskan Island

## The Life of an Alutiiq Healer

Joanne B. Mulcahy

FOREWORD BY GORDON L. PULLAR

The University of Georgia Press    Athens & London

Published by the University of Georgia Press
Athens, Georgia 30602
© 2001 by Joanne B. Mulcahy
Designed by Kathi Dailey Morgan
Set in 10.5 on 15.5 Fairfield Light by G & S Typesetters
Printed and bound by Maple-Vail
The paper in this book meets the guidelines for
permanence and durability of the Committee on
Production Guidelines for Book Longevity of the
Council on Library Resources.

Printed in the United States of America
05   04   03   02   01   C   5   4   3   2   1

Library of Congress Cataloging-in-Publication Data

Mulcahy, Joanne B., 1954–

    Birth and rebirth on an Alaskan island : the life of
an Alutiiq healer / Joanne B. Mulcahy ; foreword by
Gordon L. Pullar.

        p. cm.

    Includes bibliographical references and index.

    ISBN 0-8203-2253-9 (alk. paper)

    1. Peterson, Mary.   2. Pacific Gulf Yupik women—
Alaska—Kodiak Island—Biography.   3. Indian
women healers—Alaska—Kodiak Island—Biography.

    4. Midwives—Alaska—Kodiak Island—Biography.

    5. Pacific Gulf Yupik Eskimos—Social life and customs.

    6. Kodiak Island (Alaska)—Social life and customs.

    I. Title.

E99.E7 M87 2001

979.8′4—dc21

[B]          00-036881

British Library Cataloging-in-Publication Data available

This book is dedicated to

the Kodiak midwives and

Community Health Aides

# Contents

# *Foreword*

GORDON L. PULLAR

On September 26, 1916, my grandmother Afanasiia gave birth to my mother, Olga, in the Alutiiq village of Woody Island, Alaska, a mile off the shore of the much larger Kodiak Island. There were no hospitals and no medical doctors in the village, at least as we know them today. Nevertheless, a capable and caring person attended to the birth. Paraskeva Pestriakov (Pariscovia Pestrikoff in modern spelling), an Alutiiq midwife from the neighboring village of Ouzinkie, had been summoned. With her skilled hands, honed by years of experience, and her mind and soul, prepared by centuries of knowledge and wisdom, she knew exactly what to do.

In a time before airplanes and powerboats, Paraskeva's trip from Ouzinkie could have been treacherous. The distance between Woody Island and Ouzinkie is but ten miles as the raven flies but longer by water. The ocean waters between the two villages are dangerous and sometimes unforgiving, especially for someone in a small wooden dory. What kind of dedication and sense of obligation drove Paraskeva to make this perilous trip to tend to a childbirth in another village? Was it something she did routinely? Or was it because she was a relative of my grandmother, Afanasiia? (Afanasiia's mother was Sophiia Pestriakov.) I will probably never know. I do know, however, that I have developed a wonderment as I listen to elders speak of Paraskeva with a high respect and a distinct awe. Whatever her motivation, her trip over eighty years ago becomes personal to me when I realize that if she had not undertaken this hazardous journey, my mother might not have survived birth and would not have been able to give birth to me twenty-eight years later.

Alutiiq people taking care of their own health needs was not new, even in 1916. The indigenous people of Kodiak Island have lived there for as long as eight thousand years. Evidence suggests that overall they were quite healthy and prosperous, although there must have been some health problems. There were people treating the sick and, of course, someone had to have been there to help with the birthing of babies. Somehow, it seems, people were taking care of themselves and their families without what we now consider the wonders of modern medicine.

The world of the Alutiiq people, however, was turned upside down after the first Russian stronghold was established on Kodiak Island in 1784. Brutal atrocities by the Russian fur hunters were followed by epidemics of previously unknown, deadly diseases. The Alutiiq people would be under Russian rule for just eight decades and then, almost unbelievably, their world was shaken again. The United States bought the occupation rights to Alaska in 1867, and another new and alien system was imposed on the Alutiiqs. Through it all, the Alutiiqs managed to keep their identity and care for themselves. The Russians brought new and different methods of health care, as did the Americans after them. In many cases, especially in the treatment of the "new" diseases, this care had some effectiveness. Yet, the Alutiiqs had health care and healing methods of their own that were never discarded.

The century after Alaska came under American control presented many difficulties for Alaska Natives. The American system did not begin with a tolerance of Alutiiq beliefs and practices. Most Alutiiq people were bilingual at this time, and children were punished for speaking either Alutiiq or Russian in school. Any health care outside the known Western model was considered ineffective. Through it all, however, the traditional healers continued their work well into the twentieth century.

In 1983, I was appointed president of the Kodiak Area Native Association (KANA), an organization governed by the seven tribal authorities on Kodiak Island, and different kinds of health problems confronted us all. Since its first government contract in 1975, KANA had assumed responsibility for a wide range of programs for Native healthcare, education, and social services. By 1983, it had grown from having virtually no budget and staff to a complex organization with a staff of seventy people and an annual budget approaching three million dollars. Sadly though, KANA was in the midst of the most serious crisis of its short history. It was a time of turmoil among the island's Alutiiq people as they struggled for control of the new corporations established under the 1971 Alaska Native Claims Settlement Act. The regional ANCSA corporation, Koniag, Inc., and the village corporations were deeply divided and had resorted to the very Western method of settling disputes—by litigation. In a brief time, lifelong friends and close family members found themselves opposing each other in bitter legal battles. By then, the fighting that had nearly paralyzed the ANCSA corporations and had spilled over into KANA. The organization's future looked bleak and its very survival was in doubt. Many staff members had resigned and others were terminated as fighting intensified. Government agencies were threatening to withdraw the financial support crucial to providing badly needed services to the people. The health of our culture, the health of our communities, and the health of our institutions was in doubt. As an institution central to the lives of Kodiak Island Alutiiqs, KANA's ailments were of great concern.

How was I to possibly lead the organization through this crisis and return the focus to our important responsibilities, especially badly needed health care? I didn't know, but I was determined to give it my best effort. Elders, many of whom had steered clear of the conflicts, told me that the fighting was caused by a lack of tribal identity and cohesion. Many people were no longer thinking in terms of what was best for their people as a group but in terms of what their personal gains would be. Taking the elders' wisdom very seriously, we began seeking ways to incorporate aspects of culture and traditional values into all of KANA's programs. It was a slow process at first, but interest increased and by the end of the 1980s there was a true cultural revitalization movement underway. But it was not without periods of pain.

The last two decades of the twentieth century saw intense revelations about the conditions of Alaska's Native people. A 1988 Anchorage Daily News series called "A People in Peril" received national attention and won a Pulitzer Prize. The report described the deplorable conditions in Alaska Native villages. When the series was released, I was the chairman of the Alaska Federation of Natives Human Resource Board, made of KANA and its regional counterparts across Alaska. Taking advantage of the issues being in the public eye, and on the advice of Senator Daniel Inouye, chairman of the Senate Select Committee on Indian Affairs, AFN began lobbying Congress to take action. Senator Inouye strongly suggested that we compile statistical data that would provide Congress with some solid information on which to base decisions. The result was the AFN report *A Call to Action*. This report revealed shockingly high rates of self-destructive behavior in village Alaska.

The report provided statistical data documenting conditions of which we were already painfully aware.

Because of a lack of infrastructure in small communities, most of the village-based service providers were KANA employees. These included the Community Health Aides and the Village Public Safety Officers, or VPSOs. In the small Kodiak Island Alutiiq village of Akhiok, the VPSO in the mid-1980s was a young man named Bobby Simeonoff. He was the mayor of the village and a leader in trying to improve the quality of life for village residents. He was active in the implementation of a KANA-sponsored mariculture project, an experiment in growing scallops in captivity as a potential means of economic development for the small, remote community. As a member of the KANA staff, he was well liked and respected by his co-workers. So, when Bobby Simeonoff committed suicide, the shocking problems village people were facing became all the more real to those of us not living in villages. There was sadness throughout the KANA offices on hearing the news of Bobby's death. But I'm sure the sadness could not compare to that felt by his mother, Mary Peterson.

The health-care systems brought to the Kodiak Island villages have changed dramatically in the past few decades. We have seen the marvels of modern medicine. And we have come to accept and believe that modern medicine is the correct, and indeed the *only*, way to treat illness and provide other health care. Our collective short memories are apt not to take into account the other ways of treating people's sicknesses, injuries, and other health needs. These ways are rooted in thousands of years of accumulated knowledge and imbedded in the very souls of indigenous people. These were the traditional ways passed on from generation to generation through the millennia.

In the Kodiak Island area, even through the Russian period and well into the twentieth century, traditional healers played a central role in village health. There are still a few of these incredible people remaining, but they are elderly and no longer play the important role they once did. Yet, in some cases throughout Alaska we have seen the health-care systems come full circle. Modern medical practitioners are now turning to traditional healers in search of knowledge and wisdom. This wisdom and ability to heal is well known among Alutiiq elders. I have been conducting oral-history interviews with Alutiiq elders, and the pictures their words have painted have enabled me to gain a new appreciation for these healers. They were considered special people, in some ways even magical and mystical. Above all, it was to them that village residents turned with trust and confidence in time of illness, injury, or childbirth.

The traditional Alutiiq healers quietly and competently went about providing health care and delivering thousands of babies in the villages of Kodiak Island, even after they were devalued by ruling government authorities. I have now begun to understand their tremendous contributions and truly appreciate their significance. Much of what I have learned is from the work of Joanne Mulcahy, a caring and dedicated researcher, who has taken on the important task of making certain that the lives of the healing women, the midwives, are not forgotten. In this book, Joanne Mulcahy focuses on the life of one Alutiiq midwife, Mary Peterson, from the village of Akhiok. Like Paraskeva Pestriakov and countless others before her, Mary Peterson played a unique and crucial role in the survival of Alutiiq people and their culture. Her knowledge and wisdom connects us with our ancestors from a distant time. She is one of the *special* people.

# Acknowledgments

Many people contributed to the making of this book during the years I lived on and returned to Kodiak Island. I must first acknowledge Mary Peterson for her generous spirit, her friendship, and her willingness to share her stories. Thanks are due to her family as well, for their gracious acceptance of my phone calls, visits, and other intrusions into their lives.

Many midwives, Community Health Aides, elders, and other Native people in the villages welcomed me into their homes and entrusted me with their stories. I would like to thank Annie Boskofsky, Clyda Christensen, Nida Chya, Martha Kahutak, Larry and Martha Matfay, Enola and Mike Mullan, Eunice Neseth, Nina and Pete Olsen, Julia Pestrikoff, Rena (Cohen) Peterson, Freida Reft, Alice Spracher, Stella Stanley, Lucy Sugak, Marina Waselie, Nida Williams, and Julia Wolkoff. Many of the elders I met are now deceased, and I'm grateful to have known them. I'm particularly indebted to Betty and Vicki Nelson for their generosity, and to the late Ephraim Agnot, a true community scholar, for all his teachings.

Others, Native and non-Native, nourished me in different ways. Sheila Theriault housed me in Larsen Bay. Fran and Tom

Shugak provided hospitality and insight into life in Old Harbor. Gordon Pullar extended friendship and invaluable advice on this book and encouraged my work over many years. My debt to him is enormous. His work, in collaboration with the late Richard Jordan, Rick and Philomena Knecht, and Kodiak's Native elders, breathed life into the current revitalization movement. Amy Steffian of the Alutiiq Museum and Archaeological Repository read this manuscript promptly and provided advice and aid in finding photographs; Patrick Saltonstall and Darla Coyle offered additional assistance with photographs, as did Mike Rostad. Christine Marasigan transcribed the interviews and proved an essential liaison between my work in Oregon and Alaska. The Kodiak Area Native Association (KANA) assisted me in many ways; Elaine Loomis was both a friend and an important collaborator in community work with women. The staff of the Baranof Museum was especially helpful, as were many members of the St. Herman's Russian Orthodox Church community, in particular, Father John Zabinko, his wife, Maggie, and the late Father Peter Kreta. Father Michael Oleksa alerted me to the importance of Alutiiq identity.

My early years on Kodiak were enriched by Mary Ann and Mark Barham, Georgene Russell, and Charlie Sink, by my coworkers at the Kodiak Women's Resource and Crisis Center, especially Carol Lambert, and by Chip Threinen, who introduced me to Kodiak. Stacey Studebaker and Mike Sirofchuck opened their home to me, and Mary Monroe extended her inimitable hospitality whenever I returned.

In addition to my mentors on Kodiak, many others propelled me toward the study of culture. The late Steve McNabb kindled my initial excitement about anthropology; his wife, Marianne, kept me coming back to Alaska. Nancy Yaw Davis and Rachel Mason inspired me by their exemplary work as anthropologists. Mimi

Brooks extended friendship and instruction in conducting oral histories; Dave Kubiak offered a powerful model for community-based publication. I'm grateful to my teachers in anthropology, folklore, and literature, especially Barbara Babcock, John Hitchcock, Dell and Virginia Hymes, Catherine McClellan, Margaret Mills, and Saul Morson.

Bill Schneider of the Oral History Center at the University of Alaska Fairbanks offered valuable commentary on the entire manuscript. Victorie Hart of the Community Health Aide Program helped me sort through the history and proper terminology in reference to that program. Jeff Leer of the University of Alaska Fairbanks Language Center clarified Alutiiq spellings. Elaine Lawless read this work at a critical juncture; I thank Nancy Nusz for referring me to her.

Several residencies and grants supported my fieldwork and writing. I wish to thank Nancy Nordhoff and the staff at Hedgebrook, the Alaska Humanities Forum, the Jacobs Research Funds of the Whatcom Museum Society, the Sitka Center for Art and Ecology, and the Island Institute in Sitka, Alaska, with special thanks to the directors, Carolyn Servid and Dorik Mechau.

I wrote most of this book while living in Oregon, where friends sustain me in innumerable ways. I am deeply grateful to Kim Stafford and Diane McDevitt, who created a fertile writing environment at the Northwest Writing Institute, and to Annie Callan, Andrea Carlisle, Melissa Madenski, and Sully Taylor for their gifts of faith, direction, and encouragement. Judith Barrington and Ruth Gundle taught me about building community; Barbara Dills reminded me of why this work matters. Others provided long-distance support, including Alison Hawthorne Deming, Maggie Holtzberg, Teresa Jordan, Judith Sornberger, and Holly Sylvester.

My editor at the University of Georgia Press, Barbara Ras, believed in this project early on and patiently awaited its various re-births. I thank Lizzie Grossman for directing me to her.

My parents, Jeanne and Paul Mulcahy, taught their children to value language and propelled us toward writing; my five siblings, writers themselves, offer ongoing support. Special thanks go to my sister, Pat, for advice as well as encouragement.

My deepest gratitude is reserved for my partner, Bob Hazen, for his patience, editorial assistance, loving attention, and belief in me.

# Introduction

*First time by myself, I happened to be home alone when one of the girls was ready to have her baby. I guess it was one of my sisters, so I delivered her baby. It was like I had been doing it for a long time. I just knew how, you know, knew what to do, like there was somebody with me, but using my hands and my mind . . . My sister was worried, but those other people weren't in a condition to help, so I did the best I could. Only after the baby was born, after I got everything done, took care of the afterbirth and the baby, got the mother all settled down, had her drinking tea, then I started shaking and sweating all over! . . . When I think about it, it seems like I just came out of a trance or something, like it wasn't me. I always think God was using my hands to help this lady.*

When Mary Peterson, an Alutiiq elder, told me this story, I had already heard similar tales from other Native women on Kodiak Island. They told of heroic midwives facing raging storms to deliver a baby, of blind midwives, of the women who used herbs and plants—"medicine from the land"—of individuals who simply "knew" how to heal. The source of their "knowing" was inspiration beyond worldly instruction, rooted deep in Alutiiq culture and melded into Russian Orthodoxy.

Mary Peterson's story of healing is multilayered, following her roles as a traditional midwife, a Community Health Aide, and a village elder. She also speaks as a Native woman driven from her village of Akhiok during a critical period of unrest and social tension. When I met Mary in 1980, she was fleeing the alcoholism and violence that threatened the stability of village life. When she returned to Akhiok in 1992, she found villagers reaffirming traditional life, subsistence practices, Russian Orthodox holidays and rituals, and the community spirit that she remembered from childhood. Her story chronicles Akhiok's journey back to cultural cohesion, sobriety, and renewed self-esteem. Describing these changes, she stated, "We're finally healing."

The stories I heard from Mary and other women on Kodiak meld birth and healing the body into cultural rebirth—a collective, social healing. Kodiak's people have struggled through the last few decades of the twentieth century to revitalize a culture nearly destroyed during two centuries of colonization. As Native people throughout the villages of Alaska reclaim cultural knowledge and practices, stories of healing and renewal have taken a central place. Exemplary lives such as Mary Peterson's offer models for living to which younger Natives now turn for guidance.

The changes that have made Akhiok a place to which Mary could return happened in the twenty years since I went to live and work on Kodiak. When I moved north in 1979, I knew little about the cultural or natural landscape I would encounter. Kodiak Island lies 250 miles southwest of Anchorage in the Gulf of Alaska, the largest in a seemingly endless archipelago. Misty islands recede into the horizon, like stones skipped out to the edges of the sea. From the air, Kodiak's 3,588-square-mile expanse looks nearly uninhabited. Tundra covers the south end, and thick forests of Sitka spruce push north. The island's dense center sustains five indigenous species—fox, otter, voles, bats, and the infamous Kodiak brown bear; deer, mountain goats, and numerous other species were introduced later. Only the island's perimeter shows signs of human habitation. Over thirteen thousand people inhabit the town of Kodiak and the six predominantly Native villages that ring the island's edges. The Alutiiq people have inhabited Kodiak and other areas of southcentral Alaska for nearly 7,500 years.[1] Their recent history is marked by upheaval and population loss, but also by the survival and transformation of a rich and complex maritime culture. Waves of European and American fortune seekers, missionaries, and settlers followed the Russians who colonized Kodiak in the late eighteenth century. Russian traders, "promyshlenniki," came seeking furs in the wake of the eastward expansion of Catherine the Great's empire. They established their first colony in 1784 at Three Saints Bay, near the present-day village of Old Harbor. As the first capital of "Russian America," Kodiak also became the commercial center of the Russian-American Company. The Russian conquest wreaked havoc with the health and culture of indigenous people. After the company gained monopoly rights in 1799, Governor Alexander Baranof established outposts in Sitka, Alaska, and in California. Sending Native hunters south broke up families and further destroyed traditional patterns of life; by the time of the U.S. purchase in 1867, smallpox, influenza, venereal disease, and the alcohol introduced by the Russians had reduced Kodiak Natives from as many as ten thousand people to approximately two thousand.[2] The remaining population, once spread out over sixty-five different settlements, was eventually consolidated into seven village communities. During the Russian era, Native people became increasingly bound to working for trade goods and cash, which irrevocably altered the shape of Native life.

The U.S. purchase in 1867 increased dependence on a market economy, perpetuated erosion of cultural practices, near loss of the Native language, and a further influx of outsiders, including Scandinavian fishermen. Yet the "Creole" population that initially emerged from the intermarriage of Native women and Russian men further "creolized," survived, and flourishes today.[3] Alutiiqs have produced a unique synthesis of many cultures that they proudly proclaim to be part of "being Aleut," the term originally applied to the local population by the Russians. Contemporary Kodiak Natives, approximately a quarter of the population, coexist with a multiethnic mix of Filipinos, Mexicans, and whites of European descent, some lured by cannery work and a vital fishing industry, others by the Coast Guard or the vast surroundings of wilderness.

A relationship with a fisherman I'd met at a friend's wedding initially drew me to Kodiak. I arrived in November, when traces of red still marked a smattering of deciduous trees framed by stands of Sitka spruce. I remember my first view of the island. Against an azure sky with gentle brush strokes of clouds, the town of Kodiak unfolded. Canneries snaking down along the waterfront spewed steam. Into the crook of a snow-capped mountain's arm, the boat harbor gleamed with steel crabbers, sleek salmon seiners, small wooden dories, and skiffs. Rings of houses in concentric arcs spiraled into the side of the mountain. At the heart of the landscape, on a small bluff, the blue onion dome of a Russian Orthodox church shimmered in the sun.

Within weeks of my arrival, I found a waitress job in a harbor-front restaurant, working the 5 A.M. shift on dark winter mornings. But I wanted another way to connect to the community. Before I moved to Alaska, I'd worked in a women's health clinic and in a variety of other social service positions. I began volunteering at the Kodiak Women's Resource Center, which evolved into a part-time job. As the program coordinator, I planned community education projects and helped with the telephone crisis line. Most of our calls came from women fleeing domestic violence and alcohol-related problems. Several factors contributed to the high rates of violence: the free flow of money, drugs, and alcohol during the still thriving king crab fishing boom, a large transient population, and the often turbulent weather.

One August night in 1980, a call came from the Kodiak Area Native Association, announcing that a Native woman in her late fifties was about to arrive from Akhiok. The KANA coordinator described the woman—a respected elder and Community Health Aide, she had taught the Alutiiq language and given birth to eighteen children. Now, she fled the destructive patterns of violence and alcoholism that had altered village life. Her name was Mary Peterson.

I remember being amazed that a woman who looked so young had endured such hardships with few visible scars. I placed her in a safe home and wondered if she'd return to the village. Later, I pondered her life and her flight from the village. I had spent barely an hour with Mary, yet the contrast between her calm presence and what I imagined of her life amazed me. How had she found the courage to leave family, community, livelihood? What well had she tapped for strength? The next day, I went back to talk with her, but Mary was gone. She'd flown out on the first plane to a shelter in Anchorage.

Though I didn't reconnect to Mary then, I met other Native

women with compelling stories of life in the villages. I began to haunt the A. Holmes Johnson Library downtown, which had an extensive Alaskana collection. However, there was little documentation of women's lives, except for occasional references in the journals of Russian fur traders and missionaries or in travel accounts. Since the 1960s, feminist scholars have tried to rectify this absence of women in the historic and cultural record.[4] But on Kodiak in the late 1970s, I found little redress. This absence drove me to collect oral histories from the women I met. One of the very first women I interviewed, Katherine Chichenoff, alerted me to the theme that would become central to my research. Midway through our first conversation, I asked about the birth of her children. A spark ignited, and Katherine's tone and demeanor changed. She brushed back strands of white hair, the lines in her face deepening with joy. "Oh, the midwives! Before, they were so good. They took such good care of you. We were really spoiled. All my ten children were delivered by midwives. We never went to doctors. The midwives were so good, so clean. I don't know how they knew what to do. They just knew how to heal. They just *knew*."

In my mid-twenties then, I was unmarried and had no children. Kodiak had a sizable counterculture population and a nascent home-birth movement, in which some of my friends were involved. But aside from that, I'd had no real interest in childbirth or in midwifery. The stories opened me to the topic. Word-for-word repetitions were echoed by different women about heroic "helping" midwives and traditional healers who simply "knew how to heal." The recurrence of the same stories forced me to acknowledge the existence of an oral tradition. At the narrative center stood the figure of the village midwife attending to everyday healing as well as to the birth process. Midwifery was a calling, publicly acknowledged and religiously inspired. Many women linked healing to belief—in God, in Russian Orthodoxy, in the tenacity of Alutiiq culture, in an entire way of life built on reciprocity and tradition. Women also stressed how much better their birth experiences had been with midwives. Their insistence that "we never had problems" contrasted sharply with the recorded high rates of infant mortality. Further, women told of midwifery continuing well into the 1960s, substantially later than written medical records chronicled. As I collected accounts from women all over Kodiak, I questioned: what did those women's narratives mean in the face of a written history that ignored or contradicted their stories? How did "knowing" and "healing" function beyond literal meaning in the stories I heard? What was encompassed by "believing"? What did it have to do with "being Aleut"?

In the fall of 1981, I left Alaska for graduate school in pursuit of "knowing" and "healing" and an M.A. degree in anthropology. I returned to Kodiak every two years for the summer until 1985, when I came back for six months to complete research for a Ph.D. degree in folklore. I studied patterns in women's stories, the historical link between traditional midwives and the contemporary Community Health Aides, and the emergence of Kodiak's ethnic identity. I thought I had finished with research when a friend suggested I seek out a woman named Mary living in Anchorage who knew "all about traditional healing." I traced this woman to a nondescript housing unit on a busy Anchorage street. When the door swung open, there stood the Mary Peterson I'd met in Kodiak five years before. After we'd talked for several hours, she agreed to let me record her story.

For over a dozen years, I documented Mary's life history, her work as a midwife, a teacher, a Community Health Aide, a mother, and a grandmother. When we began, she seemed anxious to tell her story, perhaps to make sense out of the enforced exile she then endured. I wondered if she'd ever be able to return to her village. But through the course of a decade, the problems eased and Akhiok began "to heal." Through the 1980s, the cultural revitalization movement begun earlier in other areas of Alaska took hold on Kodiak. Native kayaks, traditional housing, dance, and other art forms rose phoenix-like from the ashes of two centuries of colonization. Mary finally found her way back to the windswept tundra of southwest Kodiak Island, the only place I had ever heard her call "home."

Mary's story is important for a number of reasons. First, it illuminates the cultural history of a Native population largely neglected in the anthropological literature.[5] Too often anthropologists have sought out the "pure" cultures with marked continuities to their traditions, neglecting those hybridized by frequent interaction with many different groups. Kodiak's long period of contact with Europeans and Americans lent a veneer of modernity to current social life that helped explain such neglect by the scholarly community. However, as Sidney Mintz has suggested, anthropology's "preoccupation with purity" was also part of the problem. Many anthropologists now reject the "purity" model for understanding change, looking instead to hybridized cultures and to the fluid, and often situational, nature of ethnicity.[6]

Within the sparse documentation of Alutiiq culture that does exist, there has been little focus on women. In addition to including the voices of women in the written record, a life history also raises important questions about gender and culture.[7] How do women see themselves and their history? What can we learn from their personal accounts of cultural life? How do individual stories fit with broader patterns of oral tradition?[8]

On one hand, Mary's story is representative of traditional Alutiiq women's lives. She grew up in a time when Native people still used *barabaras* (*ciqlluaqs* in Alutiiq), traditional semisubterranean sod houses, and swept their floors with eagle feathers. Her family followed a subsistence lifestyle during her early years, moving seasonally to hunt, fish, and pick berries. She maintained that life as an adult in the village, and as much as she could while living in Anchorage. As a knowledgeable elder, Mary's skills are wide-ranging. Her knowledge of herbs and healing methods is extensive. She knows the Alutiiq language, basket weaving, and the songs, stories, and celebrations of the Russian Orthodox Church. Living through periods of intense cultural change, she moved from traditional life to working for wages in the canneries, as a teacher, and as a Community Health Aide. Tragically, she has known the effects of alcoholism and violence, and the suicide of a son.

However, to see Mary as a generic representative is false in many ways. It would return us to the days of anthropological inquiry in which individuals were screens for cultural patterns and would deny as well the uncommon range of Mary's individual skills and adaptability. She displayed tremendous determination in her choice to relocate and begin again, creating a powerful role model for her children and other Alaskan women. She showed equal strength in her return to the village. Mary now serves as a bridge between traditional culture, modernization, and the current cultural revitalization process.[9]

Oral tradition is a profound force in this revitalization, with "knowing and healing" as a central part of the storied landscape. Healing is a pivotal metaphor, emblematic of deeply held cultural values and often invoked for the social as well as the physical body. At the heart of Kodiak women's stories is the concept of healing as "making whole"—the Old English root of the word. More than "curing," the banishment of illness often at the heart of Western medicine, healing seeks balance in the community or between human beings and a higher being. The anthropologist Richard Katz writes of his work in Northern Alaska, "When practiced to serve the community, healing becomes a community resource, and the community becomes a healing resource."[10] The anthropologist Edith Turner has documented similar continuities among traditional Inupiaq healers at Point Hope. She notes that in contemporary practice, "healing provides the reinforcement of connectedness, which gathers webbed strength from all its sources."[11]

Stories of healing do not deny the reality of illness chronicled by the written history of health care, nor do they denigrate the genuine alleviation of suffering certain technological advances have offered. Rather, women's stories seek to mend severed connections, splintered dreams, worlds torn asunder, wounds left gaping. Talk of healing confronts losses of the past two centuries—of population to diseases like smallpox and tuberculosis, of sovereignty, of languages, songs, dances, and of sacred and medical practices to forced acculturation. "Healing" permeates the "talking circles," which meld twelve-step "recovery" philosophy into Native spirituality. T-shirts produced for an elders' conference read: "We're healing through our culture." "To heal" is to promote Native identity, to live by subsistence, to share in a community.

Part of the healing process in Native communities takes shape in stories about healers. The Yup'ik writer Harold Napoleon offers one explanation as to why the traditional healer holds a central symbolic place in asserting Native identity. He traces many problems in contemporary life to the loss of traditional philosophy, which, for the Yup'ik, is "Yuuyaraq"—"The Way of the Human Being." Napoleon details the spirit world destroyed by colonization, in particular the loss of potency experienced by the medicine man, the "angalkuq," in the face of smallpox and other diseases. That loss culminated in the "Great Death"—the 1900 influenza epidemic. Throughout Native Alaska, cultural death incurred by forced assimilation exacerbated physical loss. Napoleon calls the erasure of culture a collective form of post-traumatic stress disorder, an "infection of the soul." Ironically, as the material well-being of Native people grew with the antipoverty programs of the 1960s and '70s, their psychic and spiritual health eroded with dependence on Western ways of life. Handed down generation after generation, the "infection of the soul" ultimately manifested itself in the suicide, domestic violence, and alcoholism that pervaded Native villages.[12]

"Knowing" is as complex a metaphor as "healing," one that I interpret to stand for the knowledge that is specifically Native, the slow accretion of learning in a traditional context. Stories of "knowing midwives" also serve as powerful symbols of resistance to outside influence—the world of Western education, medicine, and philosophy, largely male-dominated realms. In tales of their better birth experiences with midwives, women assert, "We remember a better way." The Canadian writer Ted Chamberlain has stated that "all stories are, in a way, resistance stories—saying, *this* is what we give meaning and value to."[13] Knowing is an assertion of belief—in Russian Orthodoxy, in traditional healing, in women's experience, in Native abilities to resist forced assimilation into white culture. "Knowing" and "healing" are not simple categories, but ongoing, negotiated narratives.

Mary's story thus has multiple dimensions, relating an individual's oral history as well as an oral tradition shaped in social interaction. My perspective and questions also influenced the story told to me. Life histories are "double-voiced" projects. Mary would likely shape a different life story for her children or grandchildren; they might hear her words marked by other cadences. Once I was aware of the importance of midwifery, my questions followed that direction. But I had another goal, which was to understand how women faced trauma intensified by centuries of cultural domination, how they resisted repeated attempts to deny their individual and collective identities. What I found was a resilience born of community, a marked contrast to the Western concept of individual strength. Though Mary and other women on Kodiak are remarkable individuals, they also found purpose in the collective wellspring of culture and tradition.

This book resulted from over twenty-two hours of taped interviews conducted in Anchorage, Kodiak, and Akhiok between 1985 and 1998, at a gathering of traditional midwives in 1993, at the 1998 Alutiiq Elders/Youth Conference, and by telephone in 1999. I combed the transcribed tapes for patterns, seeking what was unique to Mary's life and what echoed the stories I'd heard from other women. I did not insert my own questions, though I tried to make my presence obvious to illuminate how I moved in and out of Mary's life.[14] I have at times merged stories that were collected at different times for the continuity and shape of the narrative.

I also worked from numerous field notebooks and from letters that Mary and I exchanged, beginning in 1991. Though I missed her during periods when we couldn't visit, letters opened up the expanded universe of literacy.[15] Further, the reciprocity of letters equalized some of the imbalances in our relationship as "anthropologist and informant." In writing, each of us decided what to tell, what to omit, authoring our own lives. Letters also establish their own form of intimacy. In February of 1992, Mary sent me a Valentine's Day card, signing off with "All right, my friend, I shall write again soon." My eyes rested on her written farewell to "my friend." Living in the stream of friendship nurtures us, but to be *called* "friend" is an unexpected pleasure.

Yet our friendship is not a simple, egalitarian exchange. With grants and gifts, I tried to compensate Mary for her time, but inequalities remained. Many anthropologists have explored the power imbalances between anthropologists and informants, the people from whose stories we fashion books. Feminist writers from other fields explore a similar terrain. Teresa de Laurentis suggests that we recognize social and economic inequalities and move toward a "relationship of entrustment."[16] These are critical considerations embedded in the history of anthropology, particularly in Native-white relations in the United States. I remained ever aware of my place in the culture to be resisted—the world of Western knowledge, of academic anthropology and folklore, of people who have plundered the treasures of Kodiak's Native communities.[17] We write in a political context; knowing that, it has taken me far longer than I wanted or expected to complete this work. I worried over telling stories of social problems in the village, over the form and editing process, over the ethics of my research.

In the end, these fears paled against the importance of relating Mary's life, of making visible a person who both witnessed and helped shape "healing" events in Alaska Native history. I am grateful for the lens of anthropology in charting social change and for the tools of the folklorist in probing the world of narrative. I owe a great debt to the many women who shared their knowledge with me. But it was Mary Peterson who brought me back to Kodiak for so many years, by offering her story.

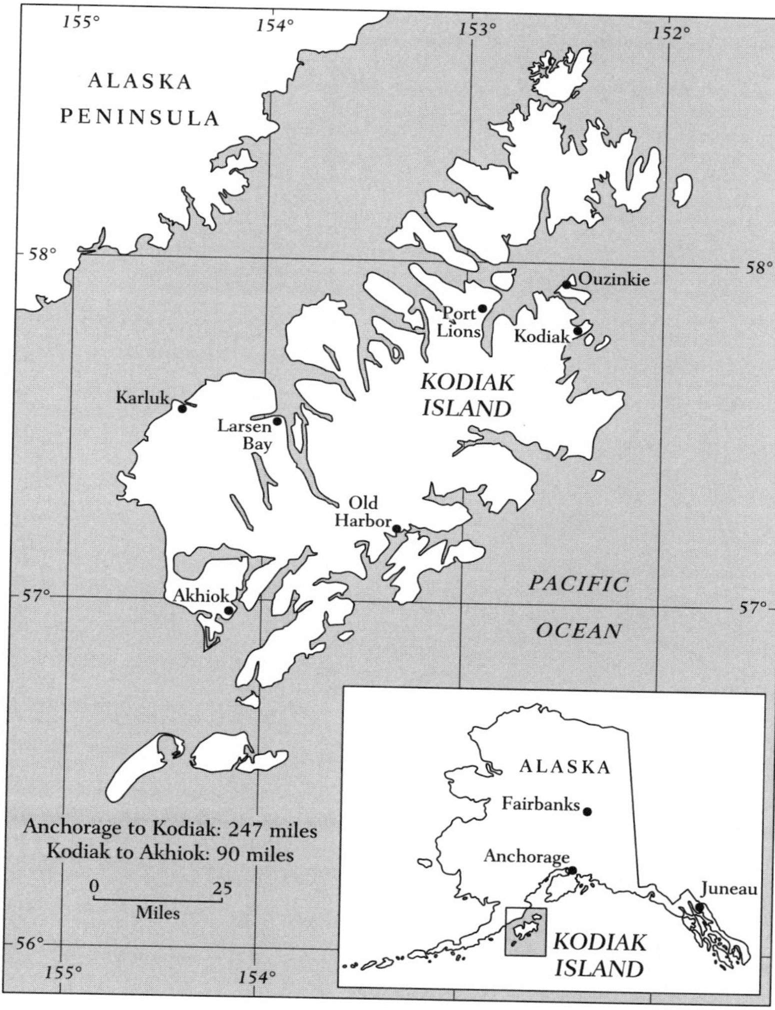
155°
154°
153°
152°
ALASKA
PENINSULA
58°
58°
Ouzinkie
Port
Lions
Kodiak
KODIAK
ISLAND
Karluk
Larsen
Bay
Old
Harbor
PACIFIC
OCEAN
57°
57°
Akhiok
ALASKA
Fairbanks
Anchorage
Juneau
KODIAK
ISLAND
Anchorage to Kodiak: 247 miles
Kodiak to Akhiok: 90 miles
0
25
Miles
56°
155°
154°

# The Early Seasons

## Family

On September 18, 1998, Mary Peterson sat surrounded by friends and relatives in a conference room of the Kodiak Inn. Outside, high clouds framed the green of Pillar Mountain on a perfect autumn day, one that might have lured many of those gathered here to their fishing lines and nets. But the second annual Alutiiq Elders/Youth Conference proved a stronger draw. "Allriluukut"— "We Are One"—was sponsored by the Alutiiq Heritage Foundation, the Alaska Humanities Forum, Koniag, Inc., and a host of other organizations. The event brought together Native people from sixteen villages and varied urban communities on the Alaska and Kenai Peninsulas, the Prince William Sound region, and Kodiak Island.

That evening, Mary's daughter Judy would arrive with a dazzling rainbow cake for Mary's seventy-first birthday, which coincided exactly with the conference. I'd flown up to celebrate her birthday and the remarkable renaissance of Alutiiq culture evident at this gathering. The regional focus made each participant witness to a larger process of cultural revitalization; collective excitement infused the gathering with tremendous positive energy. One of the most powerful events was the kinship workshop, which found long-separated cousins at the same table, discovering common ancestors. As Mary pored over census data, on the cusp of her eighth decade, she discovered she had the "wrong" name. The computer printouts revealed her "real" family name to be "Chumlumloo," rather than "Peterson," the Scandinavian surname from her grandmother's second marriage. Further, Mary's mother's maiden name, which she had long believed to be "Ewan," was actually "Signuk."[1] Mary's original reaction mirrored that of the children in her village of Akhiok; many, upon discovering that they had "other" names, clamored to change them back. In particular, Mary's children from her second marriage to Walter Simeonoff longed to reclaim their "Native" name—"Kagik." But then she reported a change in consciousness. "The kids said that changing their names would make them feel like they really belonged," said Mary. "But I told them, 'No matter what name we have, we still belong in Akhiok. No matter what your name, you were born here. You belong.'"

The place to which Mary and her children "belong" is the remote village of Akhiok, ninety miles southwest of the city of Kodiak. As one moves south, trees disappear, giving way to windswept tundra, salmon running thick along the Red River, a cannery at Alitak Bay, and this Native community of about a hundred people. The village is a kin-based world, where Mary says of the children, "Most of them are my grandkids, nieces, and nephews. Just a couple of them aren't related. Most of them are part of me in one way or another." Their lives have been shaped by Akhiok's complex history, by the hardships of isolation as well as the rugged landscape, its jagged coast and the long sheaves of grass bent seaward by the wind. The original village was located at nearby Humphrey Cove. In the early 1800s, the Russians occupied the site as a sea otter hunting settlement. In 1881, the village relocated to its present position near Alitak Bay.

"You belong." I thought back to when I met Mary in 1980, mentally charting the transformations in Akhiok. In the years that I'd known her, the village had been through tumultuous shifts—economic hardships, battles with alcoholism, village suicides, and recovery from the Exxon Valdez oil spill. In 1985, we'd begun what would stretch to over a dozen years of interviews, charting the events and changes that allowed Mary to return in 1992.

Despite the tremendous upheaval, as I watched Mary waltz at the Saturday-night dance on her seventy-first birthday, I remembered what was constant: her humor, her unshakable faith, her attachment to the village, her undaunted belief in family and community—"belonging." Mary had begun that first interview in 1985 with the binding threads of kinship, narrating back through her ancestors. Her father, Teacon, was raised by Frank Peterson, a Finnish immigrant who married Masha Ewan (Siganuk) from Chignik Lake on the Alaska Peninsula. Mary's mother, Ephrezenea, was born in Karluk in 1911 and raised by her godmother after her parents died. Mary was born on September 18, 1927. She fondly recalled her early life with her family hunting, fishing, trapping, and mining at a settlement at Ayakulik or Red River, halfway between the villages of Akhiok and Karluk. Work was punctuated by games and, centrally, the Russian Orthodox calendar. Mary's memories circle the seasons; one of her first stories involves her own birth.

*What I first remember was when we stayed with my grandma and grandpa in Red River. They called it "Ayakulik." It's right before you get to Karluk—Ayakulik, then Carmel, then Karluk. My grandma's* name was Masha, and I only knew her second husband, Frank Peterson. My dad's real dad was an old Aleut, you know. He didn't know too much about white people's way of living. They lived inland, mainly, until the Russians came. My mom, she didn't know her parents. She was raised by her godmother after her parents died.

My mom had to go to Akhiok, you know, to have her baby delivered. I was born in Akhiok, and when it was time for my mom to deliver, they walked over to Olga Bay, then took a skiff to Akhiok. When it was safe enough, they went back to Ayakulik. My parents put me on a swinging crib hanging from the ceiling. I was scared! Then my dad made me a wooden crib by their bed. It was like a hammock with a wooden frame; they put canvas over it, then poked holes in the canvas, and sewed it together with bear sinew. They used canvas for everything in those days; I hardly see that around now. That was the baby's crib, and they hung it above the mom and dad's bed. My grandma said, "Let the babies sleep above you." We didn't have mattresses like we do now; we had duck feathers and eagle feather mattresses. We never threw away feathers. They must have eaten a lot of ducks then.

For the baby, they'd make a kind of pacifier from cheesecloth, with bread and sugar and milk in it, with seal oil or butter. They called it koskuk in Russian. They put those in so that the milk is not squeezing out, and they tied it with a string. From the baby, they measure the string to the wall and nail it down so that you don't have to hold it all the time. Make sure it just goes to the baby's lips. When they start sucking, they tighten the string to make it the right length. Then, when the mom wakes up, she just reaches for the homemade pacifier. If I cried, all they had to do is put that cheesecloth in my mouth. They didn't even have to get up.

The morning is what I really remember because my grandma would sit me on her lap and drink tea. Early in the morning it was.

*I would check with her on her weasel traps when we'd walk along the beach. They'd stick in the bait, then the weasel would try to pull the bait, and the stick would fall. I'd start crying, "Owieee . . ." I felt sorry for that poor weasel. That was her moneymaking, trapping weasel all winter. In the spring, my grandfather would put them in gunnysacks and ship them out.*

*My grandpa made his living by mining. Gold mining and hunting fox—red fox, blue fox, silver fox, and weasel, and bear, too.² He had a little farm. He raised mink and he would flesh them and send them out. We had a great big garden. Well, I thought it was a big garden. It must have been, because the potatoes, you know how high the potato leaves grow—my head would just barely stick out. They'd tie up a big shawl, put me inside, and pack me around. I was kind of my grandpa's favorite because I was Aleut namesake to his wife. He was like a giant. Big and tall and a great big hook in his arm. They had to amputate his arm, but that didn't stop him. He did everything, even mended nets with that hook. Every night, he'd take it off and I'd play with it. I was only three or four, and I was a little scared of him at first. He was so big, with a big mustache, and we were just small people. But I got used to him. He loved to hold me and carry me. My grandmother favored me, too, more than the rest because I was the first one.*

*We were always alone down there at Red River. Sometimes, my grandma and myself, we'd be all by ourselves in the cabin for a week. The guys were all out hunting. When I think about it now, it's a good thing that I didn't know how to be scared! There was nobody around for miles. Sometimes, hunters would visit in the wintertime. We'd be a stocking place for their hunting. They would sleep in the other cabin we called "the woodshed." For blankets, they used to get that mattress ticking, you know, and fill that with feathers.*

*For food, in wintertime, they'd salt the ducks. There was no other way they could save them—just hang 'em out, cut off a piece when they needed. Everything was salted—that was the only way they preserved it. Salt and dry; now, they freeze. They don't even clean 'em, you know, just freeze them in milk cartons or coffee cans in water. We hunted for ptarmigans and things, and whenever we could find deer, so we'd have fresh meat all the time.*

*When we moved to Akhiok, to me it was scary. All those people, and I was just sticking close to my mom. Then, I got my sisters. I'm the oldest. The ones that are living now are myself, Jenny, Annie, Anna, Arthur, Lawrence. The others died: my sisters Maria and Evelyn, Teacon Jr., Irene, Senafont, Helen, and another Teacon Jr. The first Teacon Jr. was premature and didn't live, and the other one drowned later on. I'm sorry to say that I can't remember the ones my mother had before me. She said she had one before me that died. She had eighteen altogether.*

*We lived in Akhiok until I went to school in Karluk for two winters. We moved back to Akhiok when I was nine or ten. In the village, they were real nice to us. I liked it. It was just so peaceful. Everybody just helped each other and it was just like one big family.*

*They used to go back to Ayakulik from Akhiok. We'd go for holidays. If the bay wasn't frozen, we'd go in skiffs. If it was frozen, we'd walk. My dad dressed real warm, and I'd sit on top of the pack sack. Or my mom would pack us with her bottle, food, and stuff. No, no, no! She didn't have a bottle; she breast-fed us. Sometimes, my dad would pack me on his shoulder and put my sister Jenny in front on a board, you know, all wrapped up. They'd walk from Akhiok to Karluk, then back again. My mom said my grandpa and grandma came, too. They didn't trust my dad; they thought he was too young to be handling small babies. My grandma would take over handling me. My mom and dad were like that, too, when my first child was born.*

They didn't trust me. They raised my two older kids. They didn't let me stay with my husband, even. They thought they were getting rid of one child, but they gained two more. I hardly know taking care of my two older kids; my mom and dad took care of them.

It gets so bad in winter down home in Akhiok it's just impossible to go anywhere unless you go on land. It was hard to keep warm, too. But before, it was harder. I remember my grandma telling stories to my mom and me about what they used to do and how it was. By my mom's generation, they had easier ways to cut wood. For my grandma, they had to walk along the beach and cut the wood right where they find it, then carry it back. It was really hard to keep warm. In the summertime, they'd be busy when they're not fishing trying to get wood. They had great big sheds with the roof completely covered so snow couldn't get in. Already chopped or in blocks, there were just rows and rows of wood. We had to have lots of wood for cooking and for the banya (steam bath).

Then the cannery in Alitak started bringing coal. Some of them didn't like it because it was so messy. Ashes just build up and you have to clean it out every day, or even twice a day. Then it started getting easier when we got oil stoves. They keep you warm. And we always made little houses with low ceilings so that we'd have more heat. After my grandma died, my grandpa didn't stay in Red River anymore. We moved to Akhiok, and he went back and forth to the Karluk beach, seining. In the spring after Easter, they'd go back to Ayakulik to go fishing. We fished in winter, too. They'd cut a hole in the lake and cover it, then poke something in with a hook at the end. We'd have fish all winter. Springtime, after Easter, they'd get subsistence fish for smoking and salting, whatever they could catch before commercial fishing started. Sometime in June, salmon starts. They'd just fish nothing but salmon. They never fished crab. They got it for eating, though. There used to be lots of fish, my dad said. They'd go in a skiff and see piles of them, take a sharp pole, and spear right through them. They just got it to eat, you know; they didn't know they could sell it then.

In summertime, we fished, but we'd seal all year-round, you know. Seal tastes better, not so strong, in the wintertime. We ate fish, ducks, bear meat—bear meat is like white people's beef, you know.

There was a barabara (traditional subterranean Native house) near Ayakulik, built for the fishermen.[3] They're just covered with sod. Some of them, if they had old nets, they'd put them over the house so the wind wouldn't blow out that grass and sod. Inside, instead of wood, they'd put dry grass on the floor, you know.

When I was nine, I spent the summer with my uncle and my dad. I remember parts, you know, like when they found a glass ball. They rolled it and let me run after it. That's all I remember, chasing that big glass ball! To me, it was real big, so I must have been pretty small when I remember that.

Other times, like in the spring, we used to get up early to be the first ones to hear the birds. You know, they go "Aieee . . ." That's how they sing, and we'd all try to be the first ones up. As soon as we'd hear them, we'd take out our dolls. We could play house, play dolls outside, and then the boys, they'd wait for geese. They'd take their little boats out and play along the beach. And Easter! Easter Sunday, they'd start playing ball. They called it "Miatzic." It's a one-base game, like baseball, only you run one way and then back. There were two sides, half the bunch out there in the field watching for the ball and the other half batting. The ones that batted the most would win.

The big guys would play bow and arrow after Easter. And summertime, we'd play dolls and boats and kick the can. We made sandboxes, just like doll houses, you know, only we used blue mussel

*shells for people. The little ones were babies. Then in the fall, it was*
*no more playtime. It was berry picking and making jam, salting fish,*
*and all of us that were old enough helping watch the kids. We'd play*
*hide-and-seek because the grass was so tall.*

## Being Aleut

When Mary describes her heritage, she states, "We're Aleuts,
you know, we call ourselves Aleuts." The simplicity of her words
belies the complexity of Kodiak Natives' culture and ethnicity. A
visitor to Kodiak today might encounter an array of different terms
for native identity: "Aleut" in the speech of Mary and other elders;
Sugpiaq Eskimo, Pacific Eskimo, or Koniag in scholarly works;
and the more recently adopted "Alutiiq" in public places such as
the Alutiiq Museum and Archaeological Repository. Created in
the 1970s by simply adopting the word for "Aleut" in the Native
language, the term "Alutiiq" was born of the contemporary cultural revitalization movement.[4] Its adoption signaled the completion of a long journey toward self-definition for Kodiak's people.

Kodiak's original inhabitants called themselves "Sugpiaq"—
"real, or genuine, human beings." Archaeological evidence suggests that they descended from people who migrated across the
Bering Sea land bridge over nine thousand years ago. During the
Koniag phase of Kodiak's culture (c. A.D. 1200–1784), hunting
and gathering evolved into a more complex social organization. An
elaborate social hierarchy emerged, with social information, family background, and a person's rank coded in *labrets*, decorative
pieces of stone, wood, bone, or ivory worn in holes cut into the
lower lip. The noble class held feasts to honor its ancestors and
redistributed wealth in potlatch-type ceremonies; elaborate sea-

sonal festivals marked hunting and fishing cycles. Semisubterranean dwellings called *ciqlluaq* (*barabaras* in Russian) housed Native families in villages of several hundred people governed by hereditary chiefs, chief's assistants, and shamans. Families moved seasonally to summer fish camps and sealing stations. They traveled for conquest and trade in *qayaqs* (kayaks, or *baidarkas*, in Russian) and *angyaqs* (open skin boats), ingenious and carefully crafted vessels. The natural wealth of salmon, fowl, and sea mammals provided varied food sources, leaving time for games and ceremonial activities.[5]

This was the cultural world of somewhere between eight thousand and ten thousand people whom the original Russian fur traders encountered in 1784. The Russians called the Natives "Aleuts," based on perceived similarities between them and a group of coastal Siberian people called "Aliutor." The term was extended to people of the Aleutian Chain, Prince William Sound, and the Alaska Peninsula to differentiate these groups from other Alaska Natives. Like the misnomers "Indian" and "Eskimo," the term stuck and was adopted by local people.[6]

Traditionally, scholars called only the Aleutian Islanders "Aleuts," while referring to Kodiak's people as Sugpiaq Eskimo, Pacific Eskimo, or Koniag, establishing links to the nearby Yup'ik.[7] When the term "Alutiiq" emerged, scholars as well as local people adopted it, and today one hears "Aleut" and "Alutiiq" used interchangeably, particularly among younger Natives. However, elders like Mary are still more apt to use "Aleut" for the Creole ancestry born of intermarriages with Russians, than with waves of Swedish, Danish, and Norwegian fishermen.

Does the terminology matter? No, declared my neighbors in the 1970s. They saw Natives dressed in Western clothes, living in houses with aluminum siding and televisions, and riding three-wheelers in the villages, and they declared the culture, too long dominated by outsiders, "dead."

Historical documents seemed to support the claim of assimilation. When Mary was a child traveling between the villages of Akhiok and Karluk, the attitude of the U.S. government toward Kodiak Natives reflected the assimilationist policies of the first half of the twentieth century. Exemplary is a report from a Dr. Orr, serving in 1913 in Akhiok: "I attribute their [the Natives'] downward tendency to laziness . . . working only enough to exist . . . Idleness and ignorance is the devil's workshop." Native subsistence practices and the sharing of resources bewildered Orr: "They consider whole and dried fish better than rice and corn, and they have little in their stores for a sick person. If you give them food, the family usually help eat it." Orr concluded: "I recommend that they be colonized where fuel, water, and fish and industries are plenty to support them, and be compelled to work and to attend school regular hours and under general supervision of a Government marshall [sic]."[8]

In 1979, to a newly arrived outsider, this erasure of Native culture seemed complete. Working as a waitress and for the women's center, I saw through the lens of Euro-American traditions. Fishermen customers told Norwegian jokes and rigged their boats with the traditional long-line gear of their fathers and grandfathers. Local schools taught courses in Russian dance; the blue onion dome of the Orthodox Church loomed over the physical landscape. Shops sold gold nugget jewelry, king crab key rings, and T-shirts that read, "It's not the end of the world, but you can see it from here." This was the fabled Last Frontier. Nothing looked particularly Native.

Further, working at the Women's Resource Center, I witnessed problems that stemmed in part from the forced assimilation of Native people and their increased dependence upon federal, state, and private agencies. "Kids should learn to do for themselves" was a frequent admonition from elders, who linked dependency with alcoholism and other health problems, conditions from which villages had "to heal." When Natives abandoned or were forced to give up subsistence for wage labor or welfare, traditional healing for hospitals, and their own languages for English, an erosion of spiritual, mental, and physical health resulted.

Mary, like many elders, remembers her difficulty in learning English as well as punishment for speaking Aleut. She describes in detail the gradual shift from home births to hospital deliveries, other changes in medical practices, and an encroaching market economy. Yet, in all of the interviews I did with women, what emerged alongside this narrative of loss and erosion was one of persistence and vitality. While Kodiak's location made it a center for trade and thus ongoing social change, the shifts were not as rapid as many believe. Prior to statehood in 1959, far from the centers of territorial control, many Alutiiq practices, including foods, health care, and strong subsistence economies, remained Native. A narrative of survival and cultural invention would come to dominate as transformations in village life and national politics brought out the complex meanings of "Aleut." By the 1980s, signs of cultural renewal blossomed throughout Alaska, spurred by the 1960s civil rights agendas, the American Indian Movement, and other coalitions for social change. In this era of pride and Native autonomy, the new term of self-reference "Alutiiq" was born on Kodiak. Many practices and components of Alutiiq identity remain central for Kodiak Natives, enabling them to survive the decades when outsiders proclaimed their cultural demise. The ability to publicly display and enact these symbols and ways of "being Aleut" constitutes health as well as ethnic identity for Native people.[9]

Shifts in thinking about ethnicity in the 1980s and '90s also influenced changes on Kodiak. Ideas about ethnic identity as "pure" and bounded, a fixed set of beliefs and behaviors, gave way to notions of ethnicity as more fluid, situational, and varied within and between groups.[10] Native identity may become more important in some settings, for example, when subsistence and other aspects of traditional life are challenged. Individual responses also vary tremendously. Kodiak Alutiiqs may identify to varying degrees with the Russian, Swedish, or other European components of their heritage, welcoming rather than explaining away that ancestry.

Like many other Native Americans, Kodiak's people have reclaimed aspects of cultures deemed "disappearing" or "vanished." Elders' stories that survived underground through years of colonization are now being renegotiated as central to Alutiiq culture. But when I met Mary, Kodiak was still a decade away from a full flowering of cultural revitalization. Her stories emerged quietly, a recitation of the central tenets of "being Aleut." For her generation, these are adherence to Russian Orthodoxy (integrated with Native beliefs; see next chapter), ties to an Alutiiq community, belief in the stories and ways of life learned from elders, the Alutiiq language, and subsistence practices.[11] Mary often narrated through the subsistence cycles: gathering herbs in "falltime," spending summers at fish camp, putting up fish for winter, and the rounds of picking berries: salmonberries, crowberries, huckleberries, cranberries, and others. Intimate knowledge of the land was gleaned from subsistence practices and from walking over the mountains to attend dances in other villages. Talk about the "way things were back home" evoked an entire worldview based on community reciprocity, resourcefulness, village governance by chiefs, and traditional beliefs and practices. All were and remain part of "being Aleut."

*We're Aleuts, you know, we call ourselves Aleuts. We spoke Aleut growing up, so I know and I never forgot it. I didn't speak English until I started going to school when I was six years old in Karluk. I had an awful time! Maybe I understood a few English words, but I didn't speak it. All I know was "hello," because when my grandpa's friends came over or when he came to the village from Olga Bay or Red River, all I heard them say was, "Hello, hello, long time no see." I knew what "hello" meant, but I didn't know what they said after that. That was my first understanding of an English word.*

*My sister Jenny and I were the only ones that could speak Aleut. The rest of them, they could understand it, but not speak more than a few words, a few sentences. It's kind of sad. Now they're beginning to be sorry. I tried to teach my kids. We had a program in the village, Miney Agnot and I teaching once or twice a week. When they get older, it's harder to teach them. I know because a couple of summers ago a Mexican lady tried to teach me her language, and I was having a hard time with it. Then I said, "Ah! No wonder my kids just laugh at me when I'm trying to teach them."*

*I wish I could read and write in Aleut. When we moved back to Akhiok from Karluk, I tried to watch them write to the priest in Kodiak, and I tried to learn. But they didn't have the patience to teach us then.*

*The Aleut language is different all over the island. In Karluk, a few words are different from Old Harbor. Most of them are mixed,*

*Russian and Aleut. It's kind of confusing, everyone's saying something different. Kodiak Island people came from all over, down the [Aleutian] Chain, across from the mainland. It's just a whole mix, you know.*

*Jeff Leer, we sometimes ask him for help with translation [a linguist with the University of Alaska—Fairbanks]. He's good. I always tell him, "Ahh! You can't talk Aleut. Your eyes are too blue." Whenever he comes to Anchorage, he goes to church and that's the only time I get to see him.*

*Long time ago, women would go pick berries, men did the hard work, and women split fish. Everybody helped each other. To me, it seemed like it was better then because everybody got along.*

*It was hard to get food, but we never really ran out, you know, because there was the land and the ocean. The only things we'd need would be sugar and flour and milk. But milk, we hardly used, only in mush and cream of wheat. We always had hot breakfasts.*

*Food was so cheap then! My goodness. For fifty dollars, my dad would bring home a skiffload of groceries. Everything in big sacks— flour, sugar, rice, potatoes. Ever since I could remember, my first cooking was making mush. We called it mush, those rolled oats. Like cream of wheat, but yellow. We made jelly or sauce with blackberries. We call them crowberries, those small blackberries.*[12] *We call it sauce now, but the younger kids say, "Mom, you should make some berry soup." We made agudaq—Eskimo ice cream. You mix them all—salmonberries, blackberries, cranberries, cloudberries and cream, maybe half a cup of shortening—Crisco—and then mix the sugar so you don't feel it. Put the sugar in and let it sit awhile, then freeze it. You'll want to pick at it all day long because it tastes so good! I don't know how they give each other flavor, with the berries all mixed up.*

*For berries, the women would go on a skiff to Karluk, way up on the hill. We used coffee cans, put them in the backpack, and filled them with cranberries or blackberries or both. They could pick berries while they were breast-feeding. I asked my mom, "What if they smother while they're bending over and picking berries?" She said, "No, they find a spot where there's berries, they sit down, and they're feeding and picking berries." That's how many there were. If you sat in one place, you could get almost a gallon of berries. Now, you walk and walk and maybe get only two cups. Our blackberry patches and cranberry patches are all done now. There's nothing but mouse holes. Those mice kill the roots of the berries. It's just pitiful to see them. Animals have food for themselves, so leave ours alone!*

*They'd get high-bush cranberries, too, then store them in wooden barrels down under the ground in cellars. They dug them in and built walls with shelves and shelves. The berries would stay cool enough, but wintertime they didn't freeze. We'd have berries all winter— that was our fruit. We very, very seldom got oranges or apples because it took so long to bring 'em up here. Same way with vegetables, but a lot of people grew their vegetables. When we lived in Karluk, we had a great big garden—potatoes, lettuce, carrots, rutabaga, radishes. They stored potatoes in the cellars, too, and they don't ruin in a dark place.*

*My mom used to use nettles for vegetables. In the spring, when they get about this high [five feet], she picked them, wrapped them in cheesecloth, and hung them somewhere it wasn't too damp. And wild parsley, we used the leaves in baked fish and soup, and in salads. They're a mix of red and lavender, mixed like they were splashed with different colors. They smelled good, too.*

*Ooh, I had to wash clothes and clean. We didn't have brooms. We used eagle wings to sweep the floor on your hands and knees, scrubbing the floor with a brush. One little spot at a time. I guess from the time I was old enough, I did everything a mother did. I helped feed the kids because we were lots by that time. My mom would be busy with the small babies while I did other chores. As my sisters grew older, they helped.*

*My mom's generation, they bought hardly anything. They used cheesecloth and put dried grass in between the layers—that was diapers. I asked my mom, "Didn't it feel itchy?" She said they fixed it so that it wouldn't. My mom said my grandma was never stuck for anything. She always found a way to get by. Later on, they saved flour sacks and sugar sacks, and those were diapers. By the time I got children, that's what we used. Pretty soon, the guys had no more T-shirts. We'd steal their T-shirts for diapers! We were getting spoiled, and now they're really spoiled.*

*Before, they used a kind of grass—a wild celery—kind of like a bottle to suck through. They were so smart. Before they had a wood stove, they didn't get stuck. They used oil drums or anything that's metal, or they'd go to the cannery and have them solder iron pieces together for a wood stove. They didn't have to order a stove from Sears Roebuck. They used everything.*

*Whatever material they had, they used for clothes. Whoever outgrew clothes would just give them to somebody; whatever they couldn't use, they just sewed 'em together and made blankets. I used to make shoes from old paper. We had to learn really early to sew our own socks when they had a hole. We made our own clothes of cotton and gingham. We made underclothes from flour and sugar sacks. We didn't start wearing store-bought clothes until I was twelve, I guess. If you didn't have elastic, then you used string. A family would gather clothes that didn't fit them anymore, put them in big bundles, and go from house to house. They'd say in Aleut, "This one wants to get smaller," or they wanted a bigger shirt. That's how they traded clothes and denim. They'd get together and make a quilt for somebody, like if a grandchild was going to be born.*

*When they got grandkids, they'd give them their clothes to make nightgowns. Especially their underwear, you know; they used those long underwear. For the boy ones, they made a nightgown out of the underwear so they wouldn't get sick and they'd be healthy and good hunters and providers. They did all those kinds of things, you know, especially for the boys. If there were no grandpas, the grandmas would give them something the grandpas wore before they died. They saved them.*

*There was one old guy from Old Harbor who used to go down to Olga Bay. I remember my dad talking about him. He was always talking about shamanics because they made his dad sick. If somebody hurt his [the shaman's] feelings, he'd do something to make them sick.[13] Somehow or another, my dad said, this shamanic got a hold of his dad's underclothes—they used to wear long johns—he took his clothes and tied the end of the legs and the end of the arms and hung them on a hill somewhere or somewhere where northeast (wind) was hitting. Then, every time that northeast wind blows, my grandpa's legs would ache. If he hung something out so the wind blew through it, then his hands would swell up. They didn't know what was going on for a long time, until somebody saw him hanging out his long johns when the winds blew—northeast rain and wind, you know. So his dad knew there was a shamanic around. Other people would try to find out; some people knew who he was, but they didn't know where he lived. Anyway, they tried to figure it out, but my dad said he doesn't remember if they ever found out where he was. My dad's stepbrother, he said, "Now, we have churches, we have priests, we have bishops, there's no more of them kind [shamans]. Go to church, pray hard, all the time, every day, morning and night, regardless of* where you are, any time of the day. He always told us not to worry anymore about the shamanics. There's churches, and bishops now. You should pray lots."[14]

Wintertime, they'd have a chief or second chief check on who needed anything, food or wood or whatever, in the village. There was a first chief who'd be teaching two others. The first chief would resign, then the second chief would take over. Sometimes, if they didn't like one, they get together and say, "We don't like him. He's not doing his job right." They'd pick another one. When we first moved to Akhiok, there was another guy named Shelikof. They took him off and put Simeonoff on. He was our church reader, and he said, "I can't be church reader and try to help people," so they picked another one, Nick Phillips. My dad was chief once, but he couldn't do it because he had so many relatives. He thought he needed to take care of them. But really he had to take care of the ones that needed help first, like needy people that are poor and the elders. Then the relatives thought they were being neglected, see? It was kind of hard.

There was also a guy that ran for the chiefs. The runner would go from house to house to tell them when there was going to be a meeting. That's what I remember, this runner would just go around. If they were going to have an emergency meeting, they'd ring the school bell.

They [the chiefs] would go check on the elders, especially in stormy winters with snowdrifts blowing. They'd help them first, then help anybody else that had needs. You didn't have to ask, "Could you help me please?" If you needed help, they'd just take a knife and help you fillet fish for drying, smoking, or whatever. Now, you've got to have money to do anything.

Today, everything is push-button. Long ago, you used your arms, your legs, your mind, and your heart, not just your finger. Now, *people want to get somewhere right away. I remember the first time a Boston whaler came up to Olga Bay, and they wanted to give us a ride. I said, "No way. I'm not getting into that thing." I had seen it coming into the bay, chuu, chuu, chuuu. When I got in, I remember my snot was just flying back. I didn't want to go, but my husband wanted to. I held so hard on to his arm!*

*Now, I remember back to when I was a child and I miss them days. Go get fish, split fish, wash them. Everybody used to be down on the beach early in the morning. Now, somebody sees you need help, and they just walk on by. "Would you help me please?" Before, you didn't have to ask.*

*Before, the old people would say, "Eat lots of fish, because that's the best food to keep you healthy." They lived all their life on fish and wild meat, you know. They used to lake-fish wintertime. They'd cut a hole in the lake and cover it and poke something in, you know. We'd have fish all winter.*

*They said that when God made this earth, he took a handful of crumbs and let them turn into fish so that people will catch them and make earnings. That is so true because there are set nets all over the bay, you know, seiners all over the ocean, all spread out so everyone can catch a little.*

*I believe what they said about why fish is good—because God threw a handful of bread crumbs in the water.*

*That's not superstition, you know.*

*The way the fish run, you would think that the first person would just catch most of the fish, but you're picking fish [from the net] and your neighbor who is nine hundred yards away, his net is catching fish.*

*God sure is wonderful! He makes sure everybody catches fish.*

*I really believe in that, and that's why they say fish is good for you.*

# Faith

"It's because I believe." This phrase suffuses Mary's story and evokes a feature central to the lives of most Natives of Mary's generation—Russian Orthodoxy. The bright gleam of St. Herman's blue onion dome in the town of Kodiak is mirrored in the six Native villages, where the majority of Alutiiq people are Russian Orthodox. Around Kodiak, daily life still swells with Russian images and words—names like Baranof Street (for the first governor of Russian America), bodies of water like Shelikof Strait, and the surnames of many Natives. Perok, a popular salmon-and-rice pie, turns up at potlucks and village gatherings. The blue onion dome appears in everything from quilt squares to children's coloring books. Classes held in church basements and at Kodiak Community College teach making *pysanky*, batik-dyed Ukrainian Easter eggs. The Russian Dancers, a troupe adorned in black-and-red Cossack-style garb, perform seasonally.

The Russian church dome is just the physical manifestation of a deep and enduring cultural influence. One scholar and Russian Orthodox priest, Father Michael Oleksa, argues that Kodiak Natives' creative merger of Russian culture with their own is what constitutes being "Aleut" or Alutiiq.[15] In particular, this synthesis reflects the Native people's embrace of the Orthodox religion introduced by Russian monks who arrived in 1794, soon after the original colonizers. The monks built schools, an orphanage, established an orthography for the Native language, and left a cultural bequest that remains central today. One of the original eight monks, Father Herman, was canonized as a saint in the Orthodox Church in 1971.

Some scholars dispute that the Russian presence was so positive, yet most agree that the Orthodox Church dominates the legacy of the Russian period. Further, religion offers a glimpse of how Native people integrated colonial influences with indigenous culture. Local people adapted Russian customs to their own, afforded the priest the status once given the shaman, and celebrated Christmas and Easter where seasonal celebrations once ruled. A 1997 Christmas card sent out by the Alutiiq Museum exemplifies a contemporary version of this integration. On the cover, an ancient stone oil lamp burns before the superimposed image of the Russian Orthodox Church. The inscription on the back reads: "Beside the lamp is Kodiak's Holy Resurrection Russian Orthodox Church, which is attended by many Alutiiq people who have combined the Orthodox faith with their own world view to produce a spirituality that remains uniquely Native."

When Mary states, "It's because I believe," she affirms not only her faith in Russian Orthodoxy, but also her belief in the abiding ways of being Native. Her description of Lenten and Advent practices illustrates how Native and Russian culture meshed, the secular folding into the sacred. Kodiak villagers continue to practice the rituals of Orthodoxy—baptism, marriage, and funeral rites; weekly services are attended by a visiting priest or the village lay reader. Christmas and Easter festivities remain central. Below, Mary describes the games, dances, and other social events surrounding these holidays. Christmas finds villagers "starring," caroling from house to house while twirling a brightly decorated, tinsel-laden star. The practice derives from a Slavonic folk tradition, "Selaviq" (from the Russian "Slavit"—praise or glory).[16] For Mary, starring is one of the touchstones for keeping alive Native identity. Closely related is the masquerading she describes as beginning "when the stars go in" on the fourth night. In this folk drama, revelers visit village homes, disguised as King Herod's soldiers "going after the baby Jesus to kill him." Writing about similar traditions in the Alutiiq village of English Bay, folklorist Craig Mishler argues that "masking is the inversion of starring . . . Starring is the sacred ritual element, masking is the licentious comic element . . . In Russian Alaskan Orthodoxy, the two are balanced against one another, much as Roman Catholic Lent is balanced against Carnival and Mardi Gras."[17]

When Mary spoke about holiday traditions, her face grew animated as she was detailing the secular climax of Christmas festivities—the New Year's Eve "Devil Dance." Blackface, old rain slickers, and raggedy clothes transform locals into rowdy devils and a "New Year" character who together oust the old year in this ritual performance. Some surmise that the drama was influenced by European folk mumming practices.[18]

Mary's description of Easter also marries secular to sacred. Strict adherence to church rules balances delight in the cycle of games and celebrations that frame the holiday. The Lenten dart game she describes, *augca'aq*, is usually played by a foursome, often men, who attempt to hit the porpoise figure (*mangaq*) hanging from the ceiling. The game allows men to simulate hunting during the six weeks of Lent, when the church forbids the practices of hunting and gambling. Also, though Alutiiq people hunt sea lions and seals, they no longer hunt whales or porpoises. The game connects them to a past when they lived completely by subsistence, a nostalgia for what Mary often calls "the old days."[19]

During my first interviews with Mary in Anchorage, she spoke repeatedly about the importance of the church and its grounding influence during her time away from the village. "I get to see a lot of my friends, people I know here, and my second cousins from

Chignik Lake . . . And when I go back home, then go back to church in Anchorage, all the churchgoers say, 'Where did you disappear to?' They know me, because I go to church all the time."

"Going home" always meant Akhiok—for summer fishing or Christmas starring and the Easter celebration, pivotal events in her annual cycle. The enactment of these events based on the cosmology of Native life and Russian Orthodoxy constitutes the "wholeness" of culture as Mary remembered it. At the end of our first conversation in her temporary Anchorage home, she lamented:

"Now it's the end of November. December will go by real fast.

"I'm getting worried: Will the weather be good when I go? I get nervous. I don't like to fly much anymore.

"Oh, when the holidays come, I just hurt!

"I can just see it, just picture it. Right at twelve o'clock, the bell is ringing. People are shouting and hollering, you can hear the Old Year going away, crying. He just chucked his old clothes and went back to church . . .

*For us, it's important because we grew up with it [the Church]. We try to keep the rules like our priest says. They used to come around once a year because they had to travel by boat. There were no planes then. The preachers—church readers—they lived in the village; they were given permission to baptize newborn babies. When we first moved to Akhiok, the reader's name was Polycarp; then, it was Simeon Agnot. Right now, it's Ephraim Agnot, Simeon's son [now deceased]. Luba, my daughter-in-law, she reads the service and a few songs that she knows. She gets instruction from Father John, and when I get home, I help, too.*[20]

*We would have church services on Saturday and Sunday. The ser-*

vice is in English now. It was in Church Slavonic before, and the ones who knew the Bible in Aleut would read. They used to have an Aleut Bible. I don't know what they ever did with that. If we had it now, we could put it in the museum.

During the winter, December 4 is a holiday. It's when the Virgin Mary was accepted into the temple. They call it our Thanksgiving. January 7 is our Christmas [according to the Julian Russian Orthodox calendar]. My mom and dad would walk from Ayakulik to Akhiok for Christmas [a distance of thirty miles]. After Christmas, we'd have dancing and masquerades.

We'd get ready in the fall. There were games like blind fool's bluff, and painting and washing walls, and getting everything ready. At Christmas, we'd go starring, caroling from house to house, singing in Aleut. You'd dress up warm for starring. For three nights, we'd start at six in the evening until we finished on the third night at five or six in the morning. For starring, some places, they feed the people, serve food or candy or cake. Kids carried bags to collect candy. We'd go every night to each home and then have a dance. I love to dance! My dad taught me how. Waltz, polka, jitterbug; those days, there was a lot of jitterbug. Long ago, I remember, they used to have nothing but men on one side and women on one side. The ladies would be curling their hair with curling irons, the kind you heat in the stove or kerosene lamp, and all you could smell was burnt hair. They'd be just getting ready. Sometimes, my mom and dad wouldn't let me go out; I'd take my dress and shoes and put them out. When they went to bed, I'd run out. I got myself into trouble.

Every few years, we'd change the dressing on the star—take all the paper off and put new ones on. The star is the symbol of baby Jesus, and everybody was trying to protect the star. After Russian Christmas, when the stars went in, on the fourth night, they'd start masquerading, going from house to house. This masquerade is like those guys [Herod's men] who were going after the baby Jesus, trying to kill him. They were killing all the babies under two, you know, but they still couldn't find Jesus. Remember when they crucified him, called him King of the Jews? Well, in the masquerade, we go from house to house, covered, just like they did looking for Jesus. They disguised themselves so nobody would recognize that they're the ones trying to get Jesus.

New Year's Eve! Everybody was shouting "Happy New Year." Those were fun days. Before twelve o'clock, they'd have a New Year and an Old Year masquerading. The Old Year's dressed all raggedy in old coat and slicker pants, you know, and the New Year's dressed up nice in a suit. Anybody could do it [dress up] that was willing to. Just put a mask on. At ten o'clock in the evening, they'd start going from house to house, but they'd be careful where children are, you know. They can get scared. The Old Year tried to shake hands with people, but nobody would shake hands with him, because he's the Old, Old Year now. The New Year, he'd go shake hands with everybody. We'd try to get close to the church by twelve. The church bells would start ringing and everybody'd be shooting firecrackers like the Fourth of July. Right at twelve, everybody started shooting and hollering "Happy New Year." You could hear that Old Year just hollering and crying! You could hear him just disappearing!

In Karluk, they used to have a dance. They'd have an Old Year, a New Year, and three angels dressed in white or with sheets over them. One of them would have a clock so they'd know when it's twelve o'clock. Three other guys dressed like devils. They'd paint them with soot and use part of a boot to fit on their heads so it'd look like they had horns. They, everybody went to the dance. The Old Year came in, the devils danced all around trying to go after the New Year. Everybody sat way up high in the benches in a big building, watching the devil go after the New Year's guards. But the guards would protect him, so the devils went after the Old Year dressed up in his big old yellow slicker pants and big belly. They really made him look old. They made some kind of whistle with two pieces of wood, hollow in the middle, and they put a piece of rubber band in between. They tied it so you could blow through it. It made a sound like someone was crying or scared or something—just a weird sound!

Then the devils chased the Old Year out, rolling him along with their sticks. I got scared when I was young. When they were poking him like that, I fainted. I thought they really killed him because blood was coming out, you know, but it was a sealskin stomach filled with red water. I don't know what they used for coloring—ketchup, maybe. They poked him and he started hollering and getting weaker and weaker and then he was just little on the floor . . . Ooh! I thought it was real. They never did that again, because the kids were afraid.

Those were our mid-winter games—masquerading, dancing, and then it would get real quiet. Everybody was lonesome, you know. But they got together every now and then in the evening—the ladies would play bingo, the guys played cards, and the kids played games inside.

January 17 is a holiday, Christening Day, that's when Jesus was baptized. The kids run up to the well and get water. That's when Jesus was dumped in the water, and all the water turned holy. We get water from the well, and add it to the regular holy water.

Everybody drinks the water, and then you won't get sick.

And I still believe.

The nineteenth is the end of the holiday when Jesus was baptized, and that's when the holidays in January are over. In February, there's a bunch of celebrations—birthdays and anniversaries. Then two weeks before Lent, it's fun time. Eating, dancing, and playing games. Guys play cards and the ladies play bingo. After that, when Lent starts, it's just quiet. No drinking, no parties on the first week. We can't play rough, and no dancing. Then, on the second week, they start playing spears. Darts is a Lent game. There's a porpoise hanging from the ceiling, and they have spears that are long and real thin. There's an eagle feather in the end so that when you throw it, it'll go straight and hit the porpoise. They use sticks for points, and there's certain places on the porpoise you hit. There's a little circle in the middle and that's three points. There's two guys on one side and two guys on the other, trying to beat each other. They have sticks for points, and they try to hit certain places on the porpoise, like the head and the tail. Then in the middle, there's a little circle, and that's three points. There's a stick holding the porpoise up, and a string tied to the stick; if you hit that thread, it's six points. They bet something, too, you know. If one sides pulls in twelve points, they win.

There's a Lent game that kids play. We called it "Atama." Everybody sits on the floor, and one person shuts his eyes. We cover ourselves with a blanket, and then that person will try to guess who it is. Like they will say, "Mary, Mary, if it's you, Mom wants you to go have some tea." We say it in Aleut. If they guess wrong, then we throw the blanket open and holler "Atama." I don't know what it means, but it's the game's name.

The men play sticks, too, two weeks before Lent starts. Two guys and their opponents face each other and they each have two sticks about as thick as my finger. One of them is burnt right in the middle, you know. The plain one is called "we" and the burnt one is called "tep"—the sticks' names make no sense to me! But they're kneeling down on the floor and singing, and put the sticks behind their back, and then it's just like, "Who has the button?" The other guy tries to *guess which stick is behind his back. If they guess wrong, they just start singing louder.*

*After Easter, after the geese come by, the guys are getting their gear ready.*

## School

The Russian Orthodox clergy who arrived in the Kodiak region in 1794 established schools during their first winter. Father Herman founded a school and a seminary on Spruce Island, near Kodiak, and a school for girls in the town of Kodiak. Mission schools followed a dual mandate: from the imperial government that local people be educated, and from the Orthodox Church that such education honor local customs and traditions. To that end, the missions established bilingual texts and educational policies. Russian and Aleut linguistic traditions ran parallel and intersected, influencing one another and allowing for a genuine synthesis of cultures among a Creole population. "Creoles" were often, but not always, of mixed Russian and Native descent, a separate social class that often combined Native socialization and European education, either in Russia or in Alaskan mission schools.[21]

From the time of the U.S. purchase in 1867 until 1884, schools in the new territory were run by the Russian mission as well as American religious groups, including Presbyterians, Catholics, Quakers, and Moravians. On Kodiak, the Russian mission dominated, though the Baptists established a mission on Woody Island in 1893 and later gained converts in several villages.

The Akhiok school that Mary attended was built in 1909 during a period dominated by the U.S. government's agenda of assimilation. At the end of the nineteenth century, then Commissioner of Indian Affairs Thomas J. Morgan asserted that reservations should be eliminated, with Indians transformed into "individualized Americans." While only Metlakatla in Southeast Alaska and a few other villages were actually reservations, the overall attitudes toward assimilation affected other Native communities. In contrast to Orthodox policies, the U.S. Christian missions and, later, government schools, promoted absorption of Native people into the Victorian world of patriotism, temperance, and Western notions of a virtuous and civilized life.[22]

Of the varied forces needed for assimilation, none figured more centrally than education. The school, the great equalizer of American life, would not only civilize, it would do so in record time. Commissioner of Indian Affairs Morgan concluded that "a good school may thus bridge for them [Indians] the dreary chasm of a thousand years of tedious evolution."[23]

The territorial government, however, was slow to allocate monies to achieve its goals. In 1884, Congress passed the Organic Act, mandating education of school-age children in the territory. However, funds were meager, with no provisions for raising money. Sheldon Jackson, a Presbyterian minister, took charge as U.S. General Agent for Education in 1885. Though a controversial figure, he also emerged as an energetic fund-raiser, maintaining schools in the absence of any other centralized educational authority. Finally, in the early twentieth century, a spate of legislation created a new framework. White students and those of mixed blood were educated in schools administered by the governor working with local school boards. The Department of the Interior held responsibility for Native education; however, missionary groups, including the Russians, continued to maintain schools on Kodiak.[24]

In Kodiak villages, schools with rudimentary supplies were established in the early twentieth century. Archival records reveal
the plight of early teachers. In 1908, an anxious teacher from Ouzinkie on Spruce Island (north of Kodiak), wrote that they had
only "very much worn first year readers and two dozen cracked
slates and some really worthless books." In addition, she apolo-
gized for writing in pencil, adding that "our ink is 'all' [sic]." From
the village of Kaguyak, a Mr. A. R. Law wrote a series of exasper-
ated letters to the Bureau of Education, seeking funds. After a
series of problems held up the Kaguyak plan, he finally decided
that Akhiok could serve a larger population, and would be a better site.[25]

The Akhiok village school was run by a Mr. Thompson, who
also administered medicine since the Bureau of Education was
then responsible for health care. Mrs. Kathryn Seller followed
Mr. Thompson. An Aleut woman from Unalaska, she was Mary's
teacher. Mary's memories of school are mostly happy, despite the
difficulties she recalled earlier with the "English only" rule in the
Akhiok school.[26] Mary's fond recall of Mrs. Seller as someone who
"was everything to us" also exemplifies the multiple needs teachers were called upon to address in village schools.

*I liked school. I wanted to be a nurse. We used to practice on each
other. When we played house, one of us had to be a nurse. The nurses
used to come around every three months or so in the spring or in the
fall when it was good enough to fly. Before, they'd come in the mail
boats that go around the island once, sometimes twice, a month.
They'd come, give shots, give the babies shots, and see who needs help
healthwise, you know.*

*When we started going to school, it would be cold in the morning.*

*My dad would get up and light the wood stove, and we'd start to thaw out! Then my mom, she'd get up and make mush, like cream of wheat, or cornmeal. And every morning, we got cod-liver oil. A nurse used to come around to the villages in the spring or fall on the mail boat. They'd give booster shots for those that needed it, and they brought the cod-liver oil. They called that "sunshine," which we don't get around here very much, you know, because it rains most of the time. They had these great big square bottles they sent to all the schools. We would take turns giving it out. I gave it out so much that I didn't want to take it because I smelled so much of it. But then the teacher would just stand there until I took it. Later, they found out that we use a lot of seal oil.*

*If I had homework, I wouldn't quit until I got it. I used a kerosene lamp for light and that was hard. That was the only time I could do my homework, after the rest of my sisters and brothers went to sleep. If I tried to do it when they were up, they'd want this or that, they'd want me to help them. I'd just put it away and wait until they went to sleep. Then I wouldn't quit until I got it right. The next day in school I'd just be dipping because I stayed up too late trying to do my homework. Mostly, we learned history, arithmetic—you call it "math" now—spelling, and reading. Those were the important things, to find out what happened and why.*

*The teachers then were so good—they were nice and calm and kind. They were just like parents, and they had patience, not like now. At that time, we were really well treated. Mrs. Seller—Kathryn Seller—was my teacher. She was kind of old already, with gray, short hair. She was everything to us. She helped people that needed food—the school got food from some program. They'd get flour, sugar, tea, coffee, beans, and dried fruit. A few canned goods. I don't know where she ordered them from, but she knew some of the people in the village who were in need because they had no money to buy food.*

*I went to school in Karluk, too, when I was only seven years old. After school, my girlfriend and I used to check on one old lady to see if anyone had helped her. She had a kind of leprosy and her fingers were all crooked. We used to see if anybody had helped her with her water cups or her spit can and her potties, to see if she needed anything fixed in her bed. I would feel so sorry for her. I wanted to go to her hands and just straighten them out! I don't know what made me think that I could make her hands straighten. I was just a kid.*

*We used to play bingo in school. The older people then never thought it was an adult game; they just thought it was a kid game. The teacher used it for number learning, to see who could recognize a number or a word or a letter. Each week, it would be a different letter so we could recognize it. They would have it on the wall or on the blackboard. We never thought of it as an adult game until we went to Kodiak. I think they got cards and something to roll the balls from the American Legion.*

*I wanted to stay in school, but the teachers didn't want married kids in school, so after I got married [at age fifteen], I stopped. I used to go visit the teacher, though, and she'd give me schoolwork to do where I left off. Reading, mostly, and math. I missed that.*

## Work

When Mary spoke about her life, she seemed alternately tired and excited, as though the weight of remembering both enlivened and exhausted her. This was especially true of work, which had demanded much of her life's energy. Her notion of work didn't fall into neat divisions between paid labor and subsistence or community work. Her desire to help others in the village, her work in a cannery, and fishing for subsistence as well as wages mesh together in discussions. Yet her life story also reflects the gradually rising importance of a market economy on Kodiak, especially in the fishing industry.

Subsistence fishing has long been the cornerstone of Native survival. Salmon, in particular, is central, both practically and symbolically, to Kodiak life—reds, pinks, silvers, dogs, and kings create a rainbow of resources. Native elders tell of walking across the Karluk River on the backs of the salmon, so thick and plentiful was the run. Subsistence fishing is closely tied to kinship patterns, with families working together on boats and at fish camps, trading and passing down permits. Some anthropologists speculate that the social pattern of a mother's brother teaching her sons to fish suggests that matrilineality, that is, descent reckoned through the mother, once dominated Kodiak society.[27]

Commercial fisheries date back to the 1860s when the Russians opened a saltery on the Karluk River. The salmon canneries that followed—five at the mouth of the Karluk River by 1889—relied more on Chinese labor contracted through San Francisco than on Natives. By 1892, half the Alaskan production of canned salmon came from the Karluk estuary.[28] Within the next few decades, an influx of Scandinavian fishermen arrived, leaving a legacy of surnames like "Peterson" through intermarriage with locals.

After the U.S. purchase in 1867, more Natives moved into processing work and fishing on cannery-owned boats. In summer, they moved to fish camps for beach seining. Through the twentieth century, other fisheries, including shrimp, scallop, tanner and dungeness crab, halibut, and groundfish fisheries, became important commercially. A king crab boom, which had begun in the 1950s, reached its zenith in 1968, making Kodiak the largest fishing port in the country. The collective catch in 1979 accounted for $73.4 million. Yet by 1982, the harvest dropped so low that a closure of the fishery followed, a disastrously common pattern of depleting resources in a "boom-and-bust" economy.

Today, the groundfish industry dominates, and fishing and fish processing continue to provide 55 percent of total employment on Kodiak. Although many Natives fish on commercial vessels, few really benefited from the bounty of these commercial boom-and-bust cycles. They are rarely employed by, and even more rarely are, the owners of "highliner" boats, which reap fortunes from the sea. Rather, many Natives continue, as Mary did, to work in the canneries, fish salmon from beach sites in the summer, and comb the waters for subsistence through the rest of the year.

Mary began working in the Alitak cannery at age ten, coordinating her day with school and responsibilities at home. Her stories reflect the shift from the hunting and fishing of her youth to an increasingly complex mix of subsistence, market exchange, and government aid in Native villages.

*I worked all my life ever since I could. The first time I worked in a cannery, I was ten years old in Carmel [near Akhiok]. I unfolded boxes that they used to put the canned salmon in. My mom couldn't work there because she had small babies at home, and her sister got sick, or she left—I can't remember. Eee! I worked all day long in the summer and in the fall, and I got fifty dollars. I ran all the way home and gave it to my mom. I don't remember what she did with it. I thought that was lots. I used to be so happy, even for five cents or a quarter. Kids now, they don't even pick up money from the floor. Sometimes, when I clean up, I pick up change and have six dollars in the end.*

*In Akhiok, I started when I was thirteen. I was up in the can shop, feeding the bottoms of cans in the reformer. The tin is flattened, you know, then you put it in the reformer. There's a chute where you put them, and it goes into the rollers, which make them round. It used to be fun.*

*When I was thirteen, I still wore a dress to work. Then, the women in the cannery that came from down below [outside Alaska], you know, they'd say, "You'd better wear pants, because you have to climb stairs!" I told them I never wore pants. They said, "Well, there are some in the store, we'll see what size you wear." So, I put them on. I felt funny at first, but then I had to get used to it because we had to wear jeans to work.*

*Everybody went to work in the canneries. Some went to Alitak, some went to Moser Bay. Every summer I worked in the cannery. Then Moser Bay stopped running, and we all moved to Alitak. At first, it was all summer long till late at night—one, two, three in the morning. All summer, and you got only two hundred dollars. There was so much fish, you know, in those days. Fish wasn't that expensive. We used to work steady. The only day we had off was Monday.*

*That was all I could do, you know.*

*We always went after school was out, right after Easter. The men would get ready to go fishing, and they worked in the canneries, too. Now [April], they're going to be doing halibut, then summertime is mostly salmon. The setnetters go to their camps, and guys that run boats get them all ready. Falltime, they're putting away food. Some freeze them in milk cartons or coffee cans in water so that it won't get freezer-burned. Mostly, though, it's drying and smoking fish for winter. It gets so bad in Akhiok that you can't go anywhere unless you go on land to hunt for ptarmigan or wherever you can find deer. Now, it's easier for them because they've got freezers. Long time ago, they'd just go out and hunt, and if they got too much, they'd just share it with the ones that can't go hunting. That was good, that they shared. That's how my son, Robert, was, whenever he'd go hunting.*

He'd get enough so that he could give to those who can't go or don't have a skiff and a motor.

I could hardly wait for spring for fresh fish. Before, the younger people always brought the first fish to the elders. That's the way it was. Any new thing they got—like fish in the spring, codfish, halibut, even seal—elders got the first choice.

After I got married, sometimes we worked year-round in the cannery. Wintertime, we worked crab, summertime, I worked in the cannery when he [Mary's husband] went fishing. I think we did good one year, because he ordered material for a house in Akhiok, and then we started staying in the village. But the kids wanted to go to fish camp all the time in Olga Bay, not far from Moser Bay. Walter's uncle left him that site—all the gear, skiffs, everything. So I just went and it was good. I just stayed in the camp and enjoyed the place. It was real nice! I didn't have to go to work everyday. That was after I got kids . . .

I liked working in the cannery, except my joints can't stand it anymore. I had to quit three years ago because I couldn't stand on my feet for eight or ten hours. This dumb arthritis! Especially summertime, you have to get up early and you go till ten or eleven at night. Now, it's harder to get a job, too. You have to call in by the first of the year.

## Coming of Age

In traditional Kodiak society, young women were secluded at menarche (first menstruation) and taught life skills by a female elder. Early observers of Native life describe the isolation of a young woman in a small, low hut for six months. After that time, she was welcomed back to her parent's home, fully initiated as a woman. Often, her chin was tattooed as a sign that she was marriageable. During subsequent periods, a woman was sequestered for only the duration of the bleeding, after which she would wash herself and return to the village.[29] This rite of passage was maintained through Mary's adolescence, though the period of seclusion was shortened. She states, "My girlfriends and me, we were the last ones who were treated like that."

Anthropologists and others have argued about the meaning of women's seclusion. The "symbolic potency" associated with menstrual blood and accompanying practices place menstruation at the center of many studies of religion, taboo, and women's status.[30] Some scholars describe puberty seclusion as a positive source of knowledge, power, sexual autonomy, or female solidarity. Others see seclusion as a sign that women are viewed as dangerous and "polluting" when blood is seen as "matter out of place."[31]

Did it limit women's power to set them apart and to blame menstruating women for local mishaps, as many of Kodiak's elders did? Or was isolation a source of strength for women, a time in which important roles were learned and ritual knowledge passed on?

Many of the stories I heard on Kodiak echo Mary's account of how women were blamed for "why the fish are disappearing," seemingly supporting the view of women as "polluting." But women, particularly the elders, may not regard these as damaging beliefs.[32] In a symbolic system, an element may be regarded as powerful without being negative. For many of the older women I talked with, following the strict path of tradition kept life orderly. Clyda Christensen of Larsen Bay described her coming of age: "We listened! That was the midwives and older people teaching us. There were no napkins in the stores in those days. We made napkins out of white sheets. They had to be white—just as white when you're done as when you started . . . And when the elders tell you, 'Stay by yourself,' when you start [menstruating], I believed the elders, what they tell you. I believed. I did it."[33] Mary voiced similar sentiments in stating, "Some of us still believe," linking this rite of passage to other aspects of traditional life and to "being Aleut." She describes menstrual seclusion as a part of life that is gone now, carried on only in beliefs occasionally voiced about why "the fish are disappearing" with "girls going all over."

*Long ago, they'd make a tent for you in the corner of the house. We couldn't see anyone. For five or ten days, they put you in a dark corner, covered with a blanket. You couldn't look at people. They didn't let you see the light for five days. If you did, you might get blind. They wouldn't let you walk around or use people's dishes. You had your own—one cup, one plate, bowl, spoon, fork, and knife. You couldn't use the others for forty days. They'd say that the old blood is coming out, you know. You had to be where you're not around men, especially. Men might get sick, or older people, too.*

*They didn't let you go out on a skiff or around fish, especially in summertime. Even older women, after they had babies, they wouldn't let them out on a skiff or go to fish camp when they're having their period. When the girls started their period, if the men were at their hunting grounds, somebody would go tell them not to come home yet, to stay. The odor of the wild animal and discharge from the woman, the blood, combine to make one of them sick—the man, the woman, or the girl. They say that the odor of the blood is so strong!*

*In the spring, why do you get a cold? Why do you get sick? The ground is thawing out. You see heat coming up. All that bacteria coming up from the ground, and we get sick.*

*That's how they felt about a woman when she's having her period because of the odor and what we call bacteria.*

*If I had TB now, I couldn't even talk to you. I'd have to wear a* mask. That's how they felt about a woman with her period. Especially the new ones, when they first start. For a whole year, they wouldn't go traveling in a boat. After a year, when they're not having their period, they could go.

We couldn't go to church when we were having our period. Now, they don't respect that anymore. They go anyway. They were really strict! Now, the old people say, "No wonder everything is disappearing. People get sick all the time because the young girls are here and there. Wherever a person is sick, there can be a young girl there and she doesn't tell anybody." And the fish are disappearing.

We don't have fish like we used to. They blame it on girls traveling around. The old people get so mad!

Some of them still believe that, some of us, some of us still. At fish camp, they always say, "Why, no wonder we have no more fish. It's the girls going all over even when they're having their period. Our berries aren't that much anymore, no more ducks, girls aren't careful anymore."

The teachers explained what might happen. My parents felt ashamed to tell me, but if my grandma was alive, she would have explained it to me. This old lady, Mike Farsovitch's mom, she sat me on her lap and explained what would happen when I start my period. She said to tell my mom right away. And she told us what might happen with the guys, you know, try to rape you or something. They said never to be around men when you're alone. Some of them are bad, they might do something wrong. My mom felt ashamed to tell me all that, but the teacher explained to us.

I think that my girlfriends and me who were in school together, we were the last ones that were treated like that, like my parents' generation. There were four of us, we were the last ones. After that, nobody would say when they started their period. They wouldn't say, you know, because they learned.

# Marriage

Mary was married at age fifteen to Willy Eluska, a man chosen by her parents. She'd wanted to stay in school, but the authorities and her parents frowned upon married students. "You can't go to school anymore. You're married," Mary remembers being told. A young woman during Mary's time lived with her husband's family until the couple could find a place of their own, but Mary returned home often. When I asked how long the marriage lasted, she replied, "I don't know. It wasn't marriage to me because I mostly stayed at my mom's or my sister's."

Willy Eluska drowned a few years after their marriage. Within months, Mary met Walter Simeonoff at a dance and was married again. A short time after their wedding, Walter left for Southeast Alaska to seek treatment for tuberculosis. Such separations, reflecting the lack of services and shortage of hospitals, were common in Alaska prior to the development of a centralized health authority in the 1950s and '60s.[34]

*As soon as a girl starts her menstruation, they married her off to a man nine or ten years older. The parents picked out the man for the girl so that he would take care of her and she wouldn't get abused. But they always lived in the same house, like a woman would go to live with her husband's parents. It was always the guys' parents if they couldn't find or build their own barabara or house, whichever. They'd go to the boy's because the girl is not her parents' [child] anymore. She's married.*

*They were kind of strict, too, kind of pickylike. They didn't want to just give their daughter to anybody that wouldn't take care of her. Our church didn't allow for divorce then. Once you were divorced, you could go to church but you couldn't have communion, and you* couldn't live with another man. It's still like that, except if the priest knows you had problems. Some of those strict things are still used in our church.

Two young people, when they wanted to get married, they [the parents] used to say, "You're too young." Grandpas and Grandmas picked them [spouses]. My first husband, Willy Eluska, was eleven years older than me. My dad married me off as soon as it was time for me. I just don't know how [her father decided on a partner]! I was old enough, but my mom didn't want me to go. I missed going to school.

I hardly even remember getting married. I was out on the mail boat, Chugiak. It used to come around twice a month. First thing I knew, I was standing there and a bunch of people were looking into the pilot's house. They were looking at me, and I was wondering what they were doing, you know. Then somebody was reading right in front of me. The pilot of that boat, Robert Vansilli, he was marrying us but I wasn't paying attention to what he was reading. I was sitting down looking at a comic book. Then this guy, he kept going like that [kicking] at my feet, trying to tell me to stand up! Then my mom and dad were waving at me to stand up.

I must have been getting married!

I stood up and I was still holding my comic book. My mom always got a kick out of that. After that, it seemed like I went blank again. I don't remember when he finished reading. First thing I know, they were all clapping and I was wondering, "What's going on?"

Somehow, I don't know, to me it didn't feel like marriage. The night we were married, I went home to go to bed at my mom's. In the morning when they woke up, they said, "Oh, who is that big kid on the floor?" Ahh! I was fifteen then.

Women, after they were married, they couldn't go to church without a hat. I still wear a hat when I go to church because I was brought up that way. If I go without one, I feel I'm not doing right. It's because Mother of Heaven is wearing hers all the time. That's what my mom and dad always told me, and the older people said, "Do like she's doing—wear your hat!" My mom wore a hat all the time, every day, all day. Her godmother told her, "Look at the Virgin Mary, she wears hers all the time." My mom wore a barrette, you know, with all her hair in. She had really long hair, and we weren't supposed to cut it after we got married. They said when you do, you're cutting your veil. I just started cutting mine not too long ago. After I got married, I didn't cut my hair. But I saw that everyone else was doing it, so I had it cut because when I worked, it was just in the way. Too much work, too!

I had five children from the first marriage. All the rest are with my second husband. We met in the village, going to dances. After we met, he left for a while for the hospital. He had TB. It was called Alice Island where the hospital was, in Mt. Edgecombe in Sitka. My first husband, too, he was in the TB hospital in Seward. I don't re-member where they moved him. Those days, it was just kind of in and out.

# Women and Healing

## Midwifery and Traditional Health Care

Steam shrouds a gathering of women in a wooden *banya*, the Russian term for the steam baths that Natives called *maqiwiks*. Flames lick the bottom of an old oil drum filled with rocks as flame red as summer's berries. The women talk of the season's catch, of news in the village, of the approaching birth. One young woman rests more quietly than the others. Against her belly, an elder gently switches a *wainiik*, a smooth whisk of willow that urges the blood of new life to the skin's surface. Talk and laughter rise with the heat, enfolding them as it has other Native women for generations before them in this ritual preparation for childbirth.

I never witnessed this scene, but I heard it described innumerable times by the women I interviewed. At the heart of their stories pulsed one narrative that shaped the others: the importance of the village midwife. When I met Mary, she echoed what I had heard from many elders of women's healing roles: how the midwives "knew," how they learned to "help," how central their place had been in the village. When I began interviews, I combed the library stacks for descriptions of healing and women's roles. Early ethnographers and explorers detail the roles of the shaman and midwife/herbalist. Before Russian contact, shamans were called upon to control weather conditions, to foresee the future, and to heal in cases that required a manipulation of the spirit forces underlying illness. Shamans were sometimes designated at birth or received the call in a dream. Some were male or a kind of third gender called "shopans," or "achnuceks."[1] Often, observers noted, the "witch doctors" or "barbers" were women, midwife/herbalists who attended to everyday healing. They had extensive knowledge of plants, midwifery, a bloodletting technique called "lancing," and other forms of surgery.[2]

With the Russians came Western medicine as well as new strains of illness—smallpox, influenza, and sexually transmitted diseases. In many ways, these proved a more potent enemy to Alaska Natives than any other aspect of colonization. To battle these infections, the Russians built a hospital on Kodiak in 1808 and trained Natives as "feldshers," a rough equivalent to modern physician assistants. With the U.S. purchase of Alaska in 1867, the purchase treaty mandated that the new government maintain at least the degree of health care that the Russians had established. But as the medical historian Robert Fortuine recounts, when the American flag went up, services all but disappeared. "With the transfer of Alaska to the U.S., the Russian health care system, so painstakingly developed, was rapidly dismantled . . . The physicians and feldshers were repatriated and the trained Creole medical assistants were no longer allowed to practice."[3]

Until the late 1930s, visiting doctors and nurses, local schoolteachers, missionaries, or Coast Guard personnel met Kodiak's often dire health care needs during measles, tuberculosis, and other epidemics. The first permanent physician, A. Holmes Johnson, arrived in 1938. He performed surgery in his den; a local hotel provided postoperative recuperation until a hospital was built a few years later.[4] As the town grew with new industry and military preparations prior to World War II, life in Kodiak rapidly modernized. The one midwife still practicing in town, Mrs. King, is said to have retired in the late 1930s. A centrally administered Western health care system was established in the 1950s; the Community Health Aide position was formalized in the late 1960s. Given these developments, non-Natives often assumed that Native healers, along with the language and other aspects of culture, gradually died out on Kodiak. By the time I arrived in the 1970s, women were delivering their children in Anchorage or Kodiak hospitals. More than one person suggested that I was documenting a long dead practice.

So reads one version of history, supporting statements about the demise of Native culture. Yet what was I to make of the stories I heard that claimed midwifery to be a part of village life until the 1960s? How could I interpret the incidents of village deliveries that were chosen, not forced by weather or circumstance, even in the 1980s?

Women's stories stressed not change, but continuity, in both Native values and practice. According to the stories I heard and to documentation by Robert Fortuine, Western and indigenous medical systems coexisted for long periods, particularly in the villages. Following the U.S. purchase of Alaska, the government largely ignored the needs of the territory. Despite the fact that a primitive Western health-care system existed, it didn't touch the lives of most Natives. "Whatever health services were available were provided in the old way by family members or Native healers."[5] The following quotes from letters written in 1913 and 1917 to the Bureau of Education also illustrate the persistence of Native healing and the government attitudes that eventually drove such a practice underground:

The people here are a mixture of Japanese, Russians, Chinamen, and Whites who chanced to pass this way. In consequence, they get disease from all races . . . The general habits of the natives would spread disease—they are not very sanatary [sic] or moral if left to their own inclinations . . . They believe in bleeding, which I have discouraged in all cases. They listen to the medical witches appointed by the chief. These witches take care of all births . . . and they work against the physicians in many ways . . . they know very little but appear very wise and the natives listen to them. If they decide that a patient will die, no one does anything and they will die for want of care.

Another teacher wrote that "the mortality among the infants, we feel, is due to primitive methods used at birth and the care of the child during infancy, of which they have little knowledge . . . Unfortunately, these people still adhere to the old native custom in having usually the oldest woman in the village attend all such cases."[6]

Even after Western physicians became available in the town of Kodiak, many women who either couldn't afford the doctor's fees or preferred the midwife continued to seek her care. In the villages, many midwives and a tribal doctor named Oleanna Ashouwak from the village of Kaguyak practiced until well into the 1950s and '60s.

Mary and other women describe how the midwives continued to provide for women. They learned from other midwives or simply from witnessing the process of birth. Often, villages had more than one midwife. Village elders appointed them or called a meeting to decide on the apprenticeship of younger women. Regardless of the initiation method, midwifery required expertise and emotional strength—it was a skill and a calling, a respected role in the community.

Women's stories accentuate preparation and aftercare as well as the actual birth. Midwives brought women to the *banyas* for prenatal care to foster relaxation and to "fix" the baby's position. To increase the blood flow, they used *taaritet*, scrubbers made of grass roots gathered from the beach.[7] Massage, heat, and the steamed alder or willow branches called *wainiiks* helped reposition the fetus, ensuring easier deliveries. After the baby was born, midwives often stayed in a woman's home, cooking, cleaning, and helping for several weeks. The sense of being supported and cared for and of establishing a sense of community through "helping" is an ongoing refrain in women's accounts.

The role of the Kodiak midwife illustrates childbirth as a biosocial construct with universal dimensions and specific cultural richness. Cross-cultural studies emphasize birth as a widely varying social process; nowhere is it considered a merely physiological event. Birth as a process is shaped and defined by our attitudes toward women, power and medical authority, and larger cosmological visions, including religion.[8]

On Kodiak, many women echo Mary's description of "knowing" as spiritual understanding beyond worldly instruction. Birth transcended human control, but through the medium of chosen "helpers" order could be ritually created. For, in Mary's words, it was because she "believed" that she learned to heal, evidenced in her story of how God's hands guided her first delivery. "Knowing" symbolizes a series of complex and often overlapping spheres. It is a distinctly Native understanding and, in the realm of health care, a specifically female one. In all cases, the "knowing" of midwives is described by elders as spiritually infused, efficient, and powerful, offering a preferred method of childbirth. Women's stories stress how much healthier people were in the past and how superior their childbirth experiences were with the village midwives.

As elements of narrative, "knowing" and "believing" operated as strategies that protected women from attacks on Native "primitivism." Outsiders were less apt to attack the Russian Orthodox religion or "God's wisdom" than they would "superstitious Natives." This is very likely an unconscious strategy. Our stories, whether individual or collective, work on different levels. We seize symbols from the collective pool, and in the everyday interactions of our lives, shape story from experience. Those stories, in turn, shape us.

Another motif in women's stories that reinforces the sense of "knowing" as some kind of "second sight" is that of the blind midwife.[9] In every village, someone tells of the old blind woman who, through acute sensitivity and "knowledge," could simply feel, deliver children, and diagnose illness. Nida Chya of Old Harbor recalls her grandmother's legendary status: "My mother's mother, she used to deliver the babies all by herself. She was blind! My cousin, Sasha Christensen, remembers her. She got nineteen kids, over seventy grandchildren . . . Irene used to tell me, 'Your grandmother used to be a great, great midwife!' She delivered babies blind."

Clyda Christensen of Larsen Bay relates a similar account. "There was my mother-in-law from my first husband, Katherine Melcoulie. She was the midwife for thirty-five years after she got blind! And before that, too, she was the midwife. But she was blind for thirty-five years and was still the midwife . . . She always used to know someone is sick, just by feeling them. By *feel*, she knew what was wrong, by feeling their pulse, up here, and then here, just feeling and feeling."[10]

Are these stories true? Statistics point to higher rates of infant mortality prior to Western medical influence on village life. Reports from village teachers document the death of children in the villages. In a 1917 letter to the Bureau of Education, one teacher wrote that there were "since last June . . . six births, two of which were stillborn, the other four dying within one year."[11] These are facts. Yet women's stories about the midwives speak another kind of truth, affirming the experience of being cared for, "helped," and nurtured in the ways that midwives provided. As healers, "making whole," midwives reproduced Native life in both literal and metaphoric ways. They brought children into village life, women through the social process of childbirth, and continued the circle of reciprocity that created community anew. Stories of Native midwifery, told and retold, maintained Native identity and beliefs through centuries of colonization. Despite the gradual Westernization of medicine, women continue to assert that "This is how it was. The midwives *knew*, and we believed . . ."

*I was sixteen when I got pregnant. It never bothered me. I never felt like it was in the way, and I never sat still. I was an active girl when I was young! I was doing this and that, playing ball in the spring after Easter, hiking, climbing hills and taking walks, going all over, eight or nine months pregnant. Now, they're only three months pregnant, and they complain. I say, "You're not even that big yet. Don't act it. Just act like yourself!"*

*Before I got married, I used to help the midwives. Maybe all my life, I was helping. Before they put me in as midwife, I used to help a lot. Ever since I was school-age, six or seven years old, when they needed someone to go to the neighbors, run and get something, I helped. I kept on like that for a long time and finally, I guess, I'd been with them, helping them so much, that I learned. Irene Agnot was one I learned from. Every time she needed something, she told me. If the midwives couldn't find what they needed, I'd have to be there. I was just their runner. I guess I've been around.*

*I was always with my mom when she had her kids, too, but when I actually did it by myself, I was scared. First time by myself, I happened to be home alone when one of the girls was ready to have her baby. I guess it was one of my sisters, so I delivered her baby. It was like I had been doing it for a long time. I just knew how, you know, knew what to do, like there was somebody with me, but using my hands and my mind. Little things, like I'd done it for years. No fear or worry, no excitement. My sister was worried, but those other people weren't in a condition to help, so I did the best I could. Only after the baby was born, after I got everything done, took care of the afterbirth and the baby, got the mother all settled down, had her drinking tea, then I started shaking and sweating all over! All of a sudden I was sweating. When I think about it, it seems like I just came out of a trance or something, like it wasn't me.*

*I always think God was using my hands to help this lady.*

*You feel like you woke up from something, like being in a trance. The girls were laughing at me because I was shaking and sweating. Then it was all over and everything was fine.*

*I did that again, too, the next time I delivered someone's baby. My girlfriend wanted me there. She was going real fast. I got the rubber mat ready and some old sheets, you know, but they were clean. Got my little tray and the silver nitrate and scissors ready. We had oil stoves then, so I put a little tinfoil over a dish and put cotton and gauze in the oven to sterilize. Before I knew it, she was ready to have her baby.*

*Same way! All those kids—I think I delivered twenty-three or twenty-four.*

*They're all big now. They're all married. I guess I was delivering when I was almost as small as they were!*

*In 1947, they elected me midwife. The village, the whole community, had a meeting. They'd call the chief and second chief. If they didn't like the midwife, they'd call an emergency meeting and elect a new one.*

*As soon as a woman finds out she's pregnant, she talks to the midwife. To check if they're pregnant, you heat all over. Without hot packing, you can't feel too easily. For the first month or two, you can't feel. At three months, you can feel a little ball. You can press down on the bellybutton and feel a heart, then you know there's something there. Oleanna [Ashouwak] taught me that. I always feel for the heartbeat.*

*You can also feel where the baby's head is. Your fingers sense it, even when they're four or five months. If you can't feel it then, their uterus is turned, so you lay them head down or put something under them so the hips will be up. Do it every day until they come into the right position, and then hot-pack them in the* banya *everyday. Hot-pack their nerves and muscles. Start from the top so they don't get too hot all of a sudden. Heat them up slowly, then go down their back. Then the muscles are relaxed, and you kind of gently rub, massaging so that the baby will get into the right position.*

*You start at three or four months [in the* banya]. *Maybe once a week—not too much. There's a chance, if the baby's too small, that the heat might make you start bleeding. After five months, then you really start the* banya. *If you're having problems like aching, then you hot-pack. It just helps.*

*That's what they said.*

*Make sure they don't get cold, because if they get cold, then they'll have blood clots and, as the baby grows, they'll ache all the time.*

*Make sure they keep themselves warm, especially their feet, because they might hurt and labor too long.*

*Back then, you'd start laboring and you'd have the baby in a couple of hours because the midwives took care of you. We use* taaritet, beach grass you pull and then pound out. They're kind of like scratchers, like "chore girls" we use to clean pots. You pick them, then you hammer them until they look like a broom—they get finer and thinner. The leafy ones, the alder leaves, we call wainiiks. You get them together in a bunch, tie them, and use them to bring down the heat [on the body]—you always have to heat the whole body. They say if we don't do that, we'll labor long.

It's true. I did when we didn't have banya. The last three babies I had, we were kind of poor, you know—no gas, no skiff, nothing to go after wood with. We had no banya. If somebody invited us to banya, then we'd go. Then my mom and dad made one, but we still had no gas or wood. So I didn't get many hot packs done, and I labored.

I labored all night.

My mom said, "I told you to make banya." "Mom, you know we have no wood." We had no wood. Nowadays, these young ones, I tell them, "If you don't have wood for banyas, you have showers. Turn that hot water on, get used to it, add more hot water and let it run from the top down. Let it hit your back for a long time." Mostly, it lets the muscles be loose. You can't let the muscles get tight.

We made sure they didn't eat salt too much because if they did, the cord would be swollen, and it might be around the neck. And food— I don't know how they knew fish was good for us. They used to tell us that, and that's why they had strong teeth. They chewed dried fish; that hard fish made the gums strong.

In Karluk, there was a blind lady. Even blind, she delivered babies!

There were at least two midwives. If they know a lady was going to labor long, then they'd send for another one to help her. You had to hold her hand and you might get beaten up! A lot of husbands didn't stay because they didn't want to get bitten and pulled and hit. But I'd *sit right by them all the time, or we'd let them walk back and forth to speed it up.*

*Before you called the midwife, you'd get all the things ready. We used sewing thread to tie the cord. We'd braid it real long, then turn it, double it, turn it again.*

*They'd call for me. If they knew for sure they were in labor, they'd put a whole sheet on the window. It was kind of a secret. They didn't want a person to know that they were having a baby or they'd be nosy, you know. If too many people knew, you'd labor long, because they'd be sitting up worrying, laboring, and wondering.*

*The ones that labor long, you can't force them. You just have to give them time. And you talk to them, you know, joke around and try to keep their minds on making them laugh.*

*This girlfriend of mine, she started laughing so hard, her water bag broke!*

*Or the midwives would give them something to make them sneeze or vomit. They're suddenly pushing, and then the water bag breaks. After the baby was born, I used to have cotton or gauze ready to wipe their mouth. Just kind of hold them down a little bit before we cut the cord, waiting until the throbbing slows down. Then I cut the cord and tied both sides. We used Wesson oil to clean the baby, then watched the baby and mother and made sure the placenta was all out, or the mother would get poisoned with that piece of placenta. At first, I couldn't do that, but I had to learn. One of my girlfriends, she just threw up! She didn't like seeing all that blood, but I had to get used to it.*

*I like helping them.*

*I just liked the feeling that "Oh, we made it!" I could just hear the baby crying, and I'd think, "No problem." Oh, I used to pray hard, hoping it wouldn't be a breech baby. I used to wonder why the midwives were cutting their fingernails, you know. I finally asked my* mom, and she said so that they could put their hands in to help the baby if it was a breech baby. And I always wondered why they filled a bowl with oil and had it warm all the time. When the baby was ready, then they'd put their hands in that oil and help. I never knew that until I watched when my mom was having her last one. That's what they did, to help feel if the cord was around the neck.

They knew what to do right away—they felt it. They put their hands in oil so the cord could slip over them real easy.

They knew what to do.

We'd stay on the first night. Then, the first three days, we'd go every morning to change the baby, bathe it, and take care of everything. We'd take turns; one would sleep and one would stay up. When one got sleepy, one would take a rest while the others stayed up so that the baby wouldn't choke. Or so the mama wouldn't let the baby choke while breast-feeding. You have to watch all that! You make sure the baby's dry, check all the time, and always have a pillow on the back.

The mothers had to lay flat on their backs for ten days. They couldn't even get up to go to the—well, we had outhouses then, and they couldn't even get up. They'd bind us with a sheet or a towel to hold the tummy in because after the baby, you know, everything is just loose. Your skin is just loose, too loose to hold your organs inside you. They say if we don't, the muscles will get weak and your stomach will be all stretched out. If your feet get cold—mine used to, and I just hurt, cramps and all. Keep your bed warm so you won't ache.

That's what they taught us.

I'd go check the baby every day until the navel dried out. We used the Wesson oil that we used to use to light up the icon on Saturday and Sunday. We'd soak it and cut a piece of gauze so that they could slip it under the cord. We changed it twice a day. They say that it [the bellybutton] jumps out after that; it comes off on the fifth day.

We had binders, you know, to wrap around the baby. You want to *be sure that they don't wake themselves up or scratch themselves. When I was a baby, my grandmother would take an Ace bandage or cut up an old sheet and wrap us like a mummy. We wrapped the arms and the whole body so that the back would be straight and they wouldn't have a big tummy. Later on, when the nurses started coming around to the villages, they told us we didn't have to do that.*

*When we wrapped them, they slept good. They said especially to do it for the boys, so they'd be strong.*

*That's what the old people used to say.*

Mary's description of being a midwife slipped easily into general discussions of the healing role that the midwife fulfilled in the villages until the advent of the Community Health Aide Program in the late 1960s. She describes memories of her own childhood as well as her practice of healing.

*Whenever anybody got sick, they'd go ask the midwife. She was like a nurse, too, especially for the children. When they got a cold, we used vinegar and water warmed up. Soak a rag and then wrap it around their feet, put a lot of socks on them, and keep them in bed all the time.*

*Same with potatoes. Just cut the potato up, put it on the bottom of the feet, then wrap them in rags, and put socks over them. When they used those potatoes, they turned real black.*

*It pulls the fever down real fast.*

*If it's real slow and the potatoes don't get black, then it's not working. For older people, they'd check, and if they didn't get black, then they knew they were going to lose that person.*

*For sore throats, they used high-bush cranberries. For an earache, just heat up Wesson oil and put a few drops in and put a piece of rag so it'll stay hot.*

*We used* mogolnik *or "Labrador Tea," I guess they call it, too, for medicine, especially for coughing and tuberculosis. You pick it, chew it, and then swallow the juice. But we can't just chew it and spit it out anywhere, you know. You have to take it out and put it back where you picked it from so that it won't quit growing, so it'll come back again.*

*I used it when I was little. I was coughing so bad, I couldn't sleep. Katya from Karluk—she was a blind lady—she told me to get some of that* mogolnik. *My mom put it in a pot like tea and gave it to me every day for three days. When I feel bum or something's bothering me, that's the first thing I think about. I take it when I go home for the summer. That's almost the first thing I do, then I feel better.*

*I guess, mainly because I believe in it.*

*People are scared if they've never used it. Like everything else, what you've never eaten, you're afraid to eat. But I've used it.*

*So I believe in it.*

*When I was a little girl, I had sore eyes, too. I couldn't stand the light. They tried a newborn baby's urine—a boy's urine. That cleared the pus around my eyes. It's sterile, you know, and clean, and the warmth is just right. That stopped them from crusting, but I still couldn't keep them open. Then it was time for my dad to go fishing at Carmel. That old lady, the blind midwife, Clyda Christensen's mother-in-law, she told my dad, "When you get behind the point where you can't see the village anymore, get a clean rag and wash her eyes with ocean water." By the time we got to Carmel, I was playing house.*

*We used yarrow for when a woman menstruates too long. In Aleut, we called them* qanganaguaq. *You pick the leaves, soak them in hot water, then put them where it is aching. It's for any kind of aches. For women with menstrual cramps, they put them right across where they're having cramps.*

I asked Mary about the differences between the births of her children who were born at home and those born in the hospital in her later years. Her preference for home births reflects her individual experience, as well as the power of the midwife as a symbol for what was meaningful to Native women—staying with the mother, "helping," and caring for her and the baby.

*You know, I had most of my kids at home. And a lot of my girlfriends had their babies at home. We were scared to go to the hospital, and maybe mostly scared of flying! First time I flew, I was nineteen, I think. "Oooh," I thought, "I want to get out of here right now." It was a Coast Guard plane. My oldest boy, Ralph, was only four. He was playing with an ax and chopped his little finger. We went on a skiff to the floatplane, and when we got there, I almost backed out. But they said, "No, you have to go with him or he's going to cry." I was so scared. I thought the plane was going to break apart.*

*The ones I had at home are living. The ones that I had in the hospital, well, they were premature. I don't know, I always thought that they [the hospital personnel] didn't care if they lived. The ones I had in the hospital didn't live.*

*I told the nurses, "You know what? All my children were delivered by midwives in the village, even down to a two-pound-thirteen-ounce baby. And she's living, and she's a big woman. And those two, Sophie and Nick, they were born in the hospital, and you guys didn't help them live." And I said, "You know why? Because you didn't stay with the mother for twenty-four hours steady."*

*I guess they [midwives] just knew what to do, especially for prematures. My sister Jennie was premature. She turned so blue and dark, but my mom and grandma made her come back. My grandma would lay her on a pillow, wrapped like a mummy, and hold her chin* up so she could keep breathing. When she got good, my grandma would pick her up and hold her, keep her warm.

Shirley, my daughter, she was only two pounds, thirteen ounces. She was just small, seven and a half months. I wasn't feeling too well when I was carrying her, and I was working in the cannery. We had hard times; we weren't doing too good in fishing, so wintertime we stayed in the cannery, working on crab. My mom delivered her, and she held her inside by the oven; she kept turning her so she'd have even heat. The next day, it was dark in the afternoon, December 4. Well, the weather was good enough to fly. They flew us to Kodiak and had her in the incubator until she was five pounds. I was so worried. I thought I was going to lose her. My mom said, "Don't worry. She's going to be a big woman." Sure enough, she's just big! She has eight kids now.

I never had much of a problem delivering. All my kids were small. My heaviest baby was seven pounds. I labored four hours or five. The longest one was Judy. With my Judy, from seven in the evening to seven in the morning. All night. I told my mom, "Please don't let me suffer like this."

They didn't have anything to keep us from getting pregnant, because it was a church rule. They said it would be sinning if we stopped ourselves from having children. They said God blesses us with children. Later, I asked the priest, and he said no, it's not a church rule. But the village people still believe it. After I had so many children, finally the nurses and doctors started bringing stuff to keep me from getting pregnant. It wasn't the old way anymore, you know.

With so many kids, my sister used to help me. My dad used to say, "See how good it is to have a big family? Your brothers and sisters are helping you, but if you were by yourself and mama wasn't here, how would you take care of them? You would never have a chance to go *anywhere." Five kids I had that wore diapers at once! One of us would bathe them, then feed them, put the small ones to sleep, and the older ones would go out to play. If they got into fights, there's no use in taking parts because we don't know [who's right]. I remember an old man told me, "Don't stick up for your kids. Don't say anything. As soon as they quit fighting, they're going to get right back together again. Just as long as they don't club each other." He told me not to take their part or anything. When they started school, I'd have to make lunch because they'd come home. Sometimes, I'd have one of my sisters or one of the older nephews stay with my kids and get a chance to visit, go to bingo or something.*

*We used those homemade pacifiers, and we breast-fed them. Later, they [the mothers] chewed the food and fed it to the babies so they wouldn't choke. Or they would crush it up to make it easier to swallow. Not too hard or soft. They knew just how much to give; they used a spoon or their fingers to feed them. After the babies started getting teeth, they didn't like the spoons because they were afraid they might break their teeth. Then, they didn't know how tough our teeth are. But anyway, they really knew how, I guess, from the way they lived. You just had to find your own way how to do it. I guess they learned from their elders how to survive.*

## The Community Health Aide System

When I first interviewed Mary in 1985, she lamented the loss of her job as a Community Health Aide (CHA) when she left Akhiok five years before. The Community Health Aide Program is a critical aspect of life in rural Alaska, cited by the World Health Organization as a model for developing countries. Originally run by the Alaska Area Native Health Service, the program is now administered through individual tribal corporations. After training, village women (90 percent of CHAs are female) act as liaisons with Western physicians to provide primary health care. Though the CHA position was created when medical care modernized, as I interviewed Kodiak midwives and CHAs, I discovered its roots in a Native health care system. Western practices and institutions have phased out most traditional healing, but links remain between the role of the traditional midwife and the contemporary CHA, connections obscured in the official histories of medicine. Following the 1867 purchase of Alaska, responsibility for health care volleyed from religious groups, military personnel, and officials from the Bureau of Education to the Bureau of Indian Affairs (BIA) in 1931. Into the 1950s, health-care providers traveled by boat to rural areas, trying to combat high rates of infection worsened by poor housing and sanitation facilities. A 1955 report described health conditions in rural Alaska as "deplorable."[12] That same year, the government transferred health care from the loosely structured BIA to the U.S. Public Health Service. By then, tuberculosis had cast a pall over all of the villages of Alaska. Local women like Mary, individuals who acted as intermediaries between villages and Western medical systems, stepped forward to help. Some of these volunteers, dubbed "chemoaides," began to administer medicines, interpret for doctors and public-health nurses, and carry messages via radio. Recognizing the severity of the situation, Congress allocated money in 1968 to formalize the system and recognize the volunteer aides. Chemoaides became the Community Health Aides. The name was chosen, an Indian Health Service history recounts, "to show attachment to the community and an emphasis on health and not just medical care. The term 'aide' is not entirely accurate because the CHA is the primary care provider in the village on a day-to-day basis. However, no alternative could be agreed upon."[13]

In 1985, I interviewed Jim Sozof, then director of the program, in Anchorage. He confirmed the connection to community as well as the difficulty of the role. "The job of the CHA in a small village is not fully understood. There is a dimension we can't appreciate. She's available twenty-four hours a day, seven days a week. To endure that takes a lot of strength. I mean, people look at the word 'aide' and think it's rinky-dink. But if you took a physician out of Harvard Medical School and stuck him in the village without his nurses and his lab and support services, he couldn't do as much as a health aide."

As of 1999, over five hundred CHAs served Alaska Natives in 178 villages. Aides range in age from eighteen to over seventy; some have a fourth-grade education, others have attended college. Each is selected by her community, then receives extensive training in preventive, acute, and maternal child health care. Since 1972, CHAs have reported to one of the twelve locally controlled regional health corporations created after the 1971 Alaska Native Claims Settlement Act.[14] As the system evolved, training was regionalized and continuing education became required. Most CHAs now become certified as Community Health Practitioners (CHPs) as the culmination of clinical training and oral and written exams.[15]

Most villages are accessible only by boat or air travel, which is expensive, infrequent, or impossible in bad weather. CHAs are therefore invested with tremendous responsibility for their communities. At the same time, certain practices, including childbirth, are deemed too "high risk" for their roles. CHAs are encouraged to send mothers to deliver in Anchorage or to area hospitals in Bethel, Nome, Dillingham, Kodiak, or Kotzebue. Yet their position grew from that of the village midwife. A careful perusal of the program's history shows the links between midwifery and the

CHA position. The Indian Health Service states that "some training staff members have noted that many health aides have mothers who were midwives at an earlier time, a fact suggesting a family tradition recognized by the village." Further, Martha Randolph, manager of the Kodiak CHA program, stresses that despite injunctions against doing so, CHAs are certainly qualified to deliver children if called upon.

One Kodiak Area Native Association newsletter described the CHA as a combination of "doctor, care giver, mother, and priest." Martha Randolph echoes this description, stating that the CHA "carries the entire village on her shoulders."[16] Mary and many of the other CHAs I interviewed fit the description. She reiterated in several interviews how "helping" intertwined healing with other aspects of community life—burying the dead, listening to elders, making the transition from midwife to Community Health Aide. But during her time as CHA, Mary was increasingly drawn into a mode where curing predominates over healing and where notions of risk and the meaning of death are defined in Western terms. She describes how fearful contemporary CHAs are of delivering babies and how Western beliefs have supplanted traditions now seen as "superstitions." But she also affirms the utility of "superstition" and laments the losses sustained with the Westernization of medicine and the new definitions of birth because of "risk."[17] Her experience and beliefs reflect the cultural complexity of the CHA role. These practitioners remain a cornerstone of village life, continuing to provide the holistic care that midwives did, even as they are trained and influenced by Western thinking and medical models.

*I just fit right in [into midwifery] and I didn't have any problems. Maybe because when I was going to school, I always wanted to be a nurse. I always wanted to help. Old people especially, I always wanted to be around them. Sometimes, they used to tell stories and tell me what not to do.*

*Ever since I could remember, I was taking care of old people, helping them, spilling their spit cans. Even if they weren't sick, I liked to be around them.*

*Just to be among them.*

*And when they died, I'd be there, helping.*

*Some of the girls I went to school with, they'd say, "Aren't you scared of that dead person?" you know, talking in Aleut. "No," I said. I felt better there. I helped make flowers and fixed the coffin. You know Anastasia Farsovitch? She was the one who always took care of the dead. Someone would make the coffin and then make flowers with crepe paper and decorate the outside with blackberry leaves or a wreath. We always kept them for three days and three nights and then buried them on the third day. People took turns staying up at night where the body was in the house.*

*I helped around sick people whenever somebody needed help. I can't really remember when I starting getting paid. I think the late sixties or early seventies. Before, they'd bring something nice, like a dress or a blouse. They'd give her [the midwife] hankies. Those were a favorite, those lace hankies they used to have. Sometimes, they'd buy them and crochet around the ends. I think later some of them started to give money, and in those days ten dollars was a lot of money! Now, it's not enough for anything.*

*We went to Anchorage for health aide training. We went in July the first time. That was my vacation. We learned to draw blood. We did it on each other. There were health aides from all over for four or six weeks. We'd learn from each other, telling each other what they used to do before there were health aides. Somebody would be there that knew how to take care of sick people. Then we knew that we* weren't the only ones who had somebody like a midwife in their village to take care of sick people. We'd be talking, and say, "Yeah, that's the way it was at our village on Kodiak, too." Kind of interesting, you know, to know that you don't see people, but they are doing almost the same things in their villages. Then we'd get excited for Friday night so we could play bingo! One of the health aides would work in the emergency room on weekends, from six to ten.

You know, our people were superstitious sometimes. They believed that when somebody's sick, like when premature babies turn blue, that comes from seeing a land otter. Or the odor of the land otter will make you lose the baby. We were really strict or superstitious. But in some ways, that was good because we stayed healthy. Like when the men went out hunting, if a baby was not born yet; when the husband came home, he had to go stay with other people before he'd see his wife so he didn't smell like wild animals. He'd have to take a bath first and change all his clothes. It was really strict or superstitious. Now, with health aides, we find out just why things happen. It's not because they said this or that or saw a land otter. Sometimes, you just get sick. But before, with superstition, whatever it was, it was good in some ways. I mean, they used to take care of each other. They knew what might happen if you don't do what they tell you to keep yourself healthy.

Another superstition that I used to hear is, "Eat lots of fish—that's the best food to keep you healthy." To me, it's true, because I believe. When God made this earth, he took a handful of crumbs and let them turn into fish so that people would catch them for food and to make earnings. When I look out at the bay and see seiners all over the place, you would think that the first person would catch most of the fish. But everyone catches a little. I believe what they said about why fish is good and about how God threw a handful of bread crumbs into the water. To me, that's not just superstition.[18]

Mary also describes some of the hardships, responsibility, and community tension that surround the CHA role. I interviewed a number of CHAs in addition to Mary: Stella Stanley in Old Harbor, Joyce Smith in Ouzinkie, and Betty Nelson in Port Lions. Watching them at work, each seemed to be everywhere at once — coordinating visitors, ordering and keeping records, caring for their families and patients. Each had stories of disease epidemics, plane crashes, fishing accidents, and drug and alcohol problems. The stress level grew intolerable in some parts of the state, and many women quit. In 1988, the health service published a paper on the crisis in the Community Health Aide Program, which led to a tripling of federal funds and a restructured program. But at the time Mary left in 1980, problems were still escalating, with little relief.

*Each year, we'd have to go [to Anchorage] to learn new things they want us to know. The doctor used to tell us, "I don't envy any of you in the villages, you know." And one of the health aides said, "Why is that?" He said, "Because you're everything. You're a doctor, you're a nurse, you're everything that all the different doctors would be." I never looked at it that way before. We call the Coast Guard if it's a heart attack, a broken bone, or a big cut where they can't handle the bleeding. But other things, we do. It seemed like when I first started it was a twenty-four-hour thing, you know. I had to be alert all the time. But then the doctors and nurses would tell us to go home at five when we're done. "Tell 'em to come back tomorrow when the clinic is open." You would think they would listen, but noooo! They always want something right now. It was so hard.*

*After the health aides started, they didn't want to deliver babies. Sophie Simeonoff was the first health aide, then my daughter Vera.*

*I was the alternate. I would help her; I kind of took over if she had to leave. And then I was the only one. After me, they [the CHAs] couldn't handle the babies. They were afraid that something might go wrong. They [the public health service] were telling us it was too risky in the village. The woman might labor long, and the baby might not make it. Then relatives might blame you. You can't do anything without somebody's permission anymore.*

*Then I was thinking, "They're getting different now. If anything went wrong, I'll be to blame for not sending her to the hospital in Kodiak, instead of trying to risk helping her to give birth." Some of the older ones don't like to go to the hospital. They're used to having their babies at home. But the new generation, you know, they'd rather go to the hospital.*

## Memories of Oleanna Ashouwak

In the first half of the twentieth century, prior to the creation of the Community Health Aide system, while village midwives were attending to births, people from all over the southern end of Kodiak sought out a renowned tribal doctor named Oleanna Ashouwak. During one of our first interviews in Anchorage, Mary described Oleanna's work, detailing an extensive knowledge of herbs, plants, and a surgical practice known as "lancing"—cutting the skin to let out "bad blood" and sucking it through a cow's horn. "When they had TB, there was a place in the thumb where she would lance, or on top of your head . . . if not enough blood came out when they lanced it, then they sucked out some more with that horn . . . Oleanna healed a lot of people. I don't know how she knew, but she just *knew*." From Oleanna, Mary learned a great deal about healing, and she holds her in the highest regard.

There are no written records of Oleanna's work, but I have a multilayered portrait gleaned from stories collected over a decade. My original prompt came from the anthropologist Nancy Yaw Davis, who told me to "ask about Oleanna Ashouwak," when I told her of my interest in women healers. I asked about her again and again, until the shards of oral tradition that surround Oleanna's life took shape.

Records exist of an Oleanna born on December 7, 1909, to a couple named Niketa and Annie; no surnames are given. She lived in the village of Kaguyak, an isolated settlement at the head of Kaguyak Bay on the southeast coast of Kodiak. The once thriving village was destroyed in the 1964 Good Friday earthquake; its residents were relocated to Akhiok and Old Harbor.

Everyone knew Oleanna as the "medicine woman." People say she came from the now abandoned village of Aiaktalik, but little is known of her early life. One Old Harbor elder, Nina Zeeder, believes Oleanna learned to heal from her mother. "Her mother was blind, but she knew what roots to use for medicine. Even though she's blind, she just knew." Oleanna married Peter Ashouwak, a man twenty years her senior, but she lived alone until Walter Melovedoff, the village patriarch, lost his wife. Oleanna soon moved in. Some referred to her as Walter's "housekeeper," but she clearly acted as a wife, helping to raise his children. Oleanna lived in Kaguyak until the 1964 earthquake, then in Akhiok for a year until her death.

Rena Cohen, one of Walter Malevedoff's children, was raised by Oleanna. "Our mom died when I was only three, and Oleanna came along and started taking care of us." When Rena was old enough, she traveled with Oleanna on her healing visits. "She started teaching me when I was about nine or ten to fix people, poke their heads. Her hands were starting to get arthritis, so she let me hold them, and then she would finish it for me. But by the time I was starting to learn, I got married and I couldn't handle the job." Rena's voice resonated with awe as well as love when she spoke. "Oleanna knew how to help people. She was quite a woman. All that she knew!"[19]

Stella Stanley, who was the Community Health Aide in Old Harbor when I interviewed her, grew up in Kaguyak, with Oleanna as her childhood doctor. "Oleanna did so much with her hands," Stella remembered. "Even when she was treating another part of the body, she'd keep her hands on the head. She took people to the *banya* for rheumatism and put grated potatoes in a sock under somebody's feet to draw out the fever."[20]

The use of *banyas*, grated potatoes, massage, plants, and "medicine from the land" link Oleanna's work to that of the midwives. She sometimes delivered children, but Oleanna was more than a midwife. She shared status with male shamans and tribal doctors like the Inupiaq healer Della Keats.[21] During the mid-1980s, Stella Stanley spent six weeks at a Native educational program in Anchorage named for Keats, who was still alive then. Her stories reminded Stella of Oleanna. "Both used their hands and their hearts to heal." They also shared the use of surgical techniques such as bloodletting, called "poking" by Keats and "lancing" on Kodiak. By the 1980s, Della Keats had garnered recognition statewide for her remarkable work, while Oleanna remained unknown outside Kodiak.

For Mary, the unique aspect of Oleanna's practice was "holding." This application of pressure to restore balance to the body's blood flow figures centrally in stories about Oleanna. Many accounts depict her seated above the patient, in the warmth and comfort of the *banya*, "holding" the patient's body.[22]

Other stories express contradictory feelings about this powerful healer. Victor Melovedoff and Willy Sugak of Old Harbor called Oleanna a "witch doctor." I was visiting the village of Old Harbor when they related stories about her practice; when I pushed for an explanation of "witch doctor," Walter backed down first. "No! She was good. She helped a lot of people." "Oh, she helped me, too," Victor acquiesced quickly. "Just with her hands. She took me in the *banya* and held me. And she used that little knife." He put down his cards and gestured to simulate a poking motion. "Then why call her 'witch doctor'?" I queried. Victor shrugged. "I don't know how she knew all of that."

One Native woman named Sasha, who worked at a Kodiak hotel, had known Oleanna in Kaguyak.[23] Sasha expressed great regard for Oleanna, but her stories also slant toward myth. Oleanna never had children, Sasha said. "I guess she was losing them, miscarriages or something. I don't know, they used to say she was getting rid of her babies herself . . . It was around '62 or '63. Her husband was in our place . . . He was talking with my adopted parents. He said Oleanna was in the *banya*, and he went out, and she let him see something. I don't know . . . She said she thought she was having a miscarriage. I guess she did have a miscarriage or something, but then she let her husband look at that. He said it didn't look like a human being, it looked like a rooster or something. That's what he was telling my parents. I couldn't believe what her husband was talking about, but I understand now. He said it's not human. He said it looked like a rooster or some kind of bird. It had wings."

How do such stories arise, and what do they mean to the tellers? Stories about women in powerful roles sometimes embody mythic rather than literal truths. Myths about Oleanna allow conflicts in collective thinking to exist without resolution.[24] Mary,

Rena, Stella, and others expressed deep respect for the woman who cured and helped so many people. These stories repeat the triumph of Native healing over Western medicine. They celebrate not only one woman's power but an entire worldview and way of healing. Other stories express fear, perhaps of being judged, echoing earlier pronouncements by outsiders. Ethnographic accounts of healers on Kodiak refer to women such as Oleanna as "witch doctors," a charge later echoed by U.S. government officials.[25]

Oleanna also existed outside the social boundaries of her time. She hadn't followed the path of most women toward marriage and motherhood; she shared status with male shamans. Mary tells of how Oleanna ventured into the realm of "untouchables" who were near death. She was deeply religious, yet she defied church tradition by going to church when she had her period. Oleanna encouraged women to seize control of their lives and care for themselves; she commanded such great respect as a healer that she had authority over men in the community. "She tells them what to do, and if they don't, she tells them she can't help them," Mary stated.

Stories about Oleanna also speak to the marginal status that healers, especially women, often hold. One view suggests that healers are positioned between nature and culture or between the world of the living and ancestral spirits. Often, healing and ritual religious roles overlap, offering dual power to particular individuals. In addition, postmenopausal women gain freedom denied those still fertile and reproducing. Stories about Oleanna may illustrate power accrued because of age as well as ritual status.[26]

Of the two conflicting strains of stories about Oleanna—as the "witch doctor," and the devout healer—neither had entered the written record. Both circulated orally, waiting to be seized, reshaped, mythologized. In *Myths We Live By*, Thompson and Samuel write that for women, for minorities, "for the less powerful, and most of all for the excluded, collective memory and myth are often still more salient, constantly resorted to both in reinforcing a sense of self and as strategies for survival. To call such stories myths is not to deny their roots in real incidents and real social conflicts."[27]

Mary did not speak of anyone else in her life with the passion she displayed for Oleanna. She remembers only the generosity and courage of this healer who cured pneumonia, tuberculosis, and heart disease. To Mary, she had been a friend and a teacher.

*Oleanna wasn't the midwife. She took care of sick people.*

*She just knew what to do!*

*It was kind of amazing, you know. She'd just take your pulse, and she'd know what's bothering you. She'd take both your wrists and, you know, hold them. Like me, when I had kidney problems, she let me stay in Kaguyak. That's when I was married to my first husband, and Oleanna was his relative. I went to Kodiak and had a checkup and they gave me some medicine, and I was kind of worried about pills. I'd always think maybe they gave me the wrong kind. So we stopped on the way to Akhiok in Kaguyak, and she said, "Why don't you stay back?" so she could take care of me in the* banya. *To her, I was just skinny and pale and looked sick. So my husband went home and I stayed on. I felt weak. I could not even make it up the stairs. She hot-packed me first in the* banya, *then she would hold my head, you know, all my pulse points. She would put her hands right here [under the chin], with her thumbs on the back [at the base of the neck]. She held it there until both sides are evenly pulsing.*

*Did you ever try holding your head real hard? Then let go real fast? She did that for three days until she got it.*

*I don't know how she knew, but she held it until she got the right beat.*

*She said that I had cold on my kidneys. For three days, she hot-packed me and kept me in bed. The only time I got up was to eat, and only soup—fish soup. She wouldn't let me eat any meat, no tea or coffee, not even milk. She let me eat cranberries. I never did ask her why, but I think it had to do with my kidneys.*

*Every day, after we had* banya, *we would sit on the bed. She would sit behind me and have me against her. She'd hold me and tell me to relax and not worry. Don't think about anything that will make your heart beat, just relax, just relax.*

*I fell asleep the first two times, that's how run down I was. I slept for most of the time. That's how tired I was.*

*I guess I was just overworked and had too many children. I was just run down from getting pregnant every year. My system was too weak to carry them for nine months. She told me not to have any more children because it was affecting my kidneys. That was the same thing the doctor told me; he said to have a hysterectomy. I had eleven [living children] then. I had five more after that.*

*She just hot-packed me, fed me, cared for me. I never felt so good in a long, long time. I think I was there a month and a half. I never had those problems again. When I went back to Anchorage to get a checkup on my kidney stones, they could never figure out what happened.*

*She really healed a lot of people! They listened to her because she was real strict about helping people. If they did what she told them to do and not to do, she'd help them, but if they didn't, she wouldn't. She said I couldn't sleep with my husband. I couldn't go visiting. I had to keep myself calm and not to worry or make my heart excited, you know. Just rest.*

*I know two people that lived for a long time after they had real bad*

TB. Walter Arsenti, she took care of him when there was just nothing but skin and bones. She healed him. Nobody would go in there, you know, who didn't like to touch sick people. That's how bad he smelled, like he was decomposed. He had tuberculosis so bad that he was just skin and bones. She told him that if he did what she asked him to do, she would take care of him and make him well. But "if you're not going to listen to me and do what I tell you, it'll be a waste of time." So she took care of him. He stayed in bed. She made him soups and herb tea. That's what he could eat, because he was too weak even to chew. She gave him medicine from the land, brewed it like tea. It looked like blackberries. She was there taking care of him all by herself, except when she had her period. I think it was her husband who took over when she was having her period. In a month's time, he started sitting up by himself and eating, and she got him back. He was in his twenties when he was sick, and he lived for a long time, into his seventies. He died not long ago.

Before, they had little knives they used to cut and make it bleed when we had headaches. Sometimes on the vein or right in the back of the neck. Oleanna did it, but as she grew older, she was too shaky. They used a cow's horn, too, and sucked on it where the pain was until it got just red. It kind of numbs it, like the kids do with a cup or a glass, you know? That's what they did so it would numb the spot where they were going to lance it. When they had TB, there was a place in the thumb where Oleanna would lance, or on top of your hand. Sometimes they cut right below the neck for the ones that have pain in their chest; I think it's what we call pleurisy now. If not enough blood came out when they lance it, then they sucked out some more with that horn. If they hit it just right, the blood comes out almost black. After a baby's born, they let out the old blood so that you could start getting your strength back.

*I learned about plants from Oleanna. She used them on my dad when he had pains. When they came to Akhiok, she would bring him some, and that's when I asked her where they're from. Sometimes, when I asked too much, she'd say, "Ah, you're asking too much!" That's how they taught people. You have to be with them and see what they're doing. Go with them when they go get whatever they use for healing and pain. It was her ancestors, I guess, she learned from. They were older people here a long time before I was born. She was from Aiaktalik, the little island not far from the village. That village is dead now.*

*She healed a lot of people. I don't know how she knew, but she just knew which side. She knew how to hold them, to get the pulse points. For heart trouble, she would wrap her arms around and hold you tight until she got the pulse right.*

*Everyone respected her, and she was an easygoing person. She wasn't rough. She was so nice and made you feel comfortable to be around her. They called for her all over. We had no hospitals then.*

*She was really something. She just knew! I guess she just liked taking care of people.*

I asked Mary about the stories I'd heard about Oleanna and people's beliefs about why she didn't have children of her own or that she had aborted her own children. She seemed frustrated in hearing these reports from others.

*Maybe, I guess. I don't know. She always miscarried. She did get pregnant two times that I know, different years. She was living with a man in Akhiok and she got pregnant, and another time in summertime she miscarried. Some of them believed that God punished her, that's why she didn't have children. People were superstitious. If a woman doesn't get children, they say she's not a good woman, that's why God doesn't let her have children.*

*She was a good woman! Most of them believed that she's doing a greater job than we are, helping the sick and helping the poor, bringing them food. Like for elder people, she would just cook them something and bring it over.*

*After the tidal wave, they moved to Akhiok. She started getting sick, and she wouldn't want to go to the hospital. She knew her time had come and she didn't want anything done. She knew what was wrong with her. They called it* amikuq—*cancer. In our language,* amikuq *is "octopus," it has lots of legs.*

*She had a touch or gift or whatever.*

*She just knew what to do!*

*She was really religious and used to go to church all the time, even when she had her period. She used to have her periods almost all the time, I think because of the miscarriages. But she'd go to church if she felt the need to go pray for somebody. I'm glad I got to know her, because I really believe in her.*

Mary Peterson, 1991

(*Left to right*) "Grandma" W. of Georgia Stream; Natalie Farsovich; the midwives Stephanida Iagosha, Alocalli, and Shelikof; and Mary Agnot, Akhiok 1928. (Courtesy National Archives and Records Administration, Pacific Alaska Region, Anchorage)

The Alitak Cannery where Mary worked for many years. Photograph by
Thwaites, c. 1900. (neg. no. 0226-6013; Courtesy Special Collections
Division, University of Washington Libraries)

Census taker with a group of Alutiiq people on Aiaktalik Island,
May 1937. A *barabara*, a traditional Native house, stands to the
far left. (Courtesy Kodiak Historical Society)

Akhiok's Russian Orthodox church, May 1974. (Courtesy Kodiak Historical Society)

Aerial view of the village of Akhiok, March 1985.
(Photograph by Nancy Yaw Davis)

Mrs. Kathryn Seller (*right*) weaving baskets
with Alice Hope in their village on Unalaska.
(Courtesy Kodiak Historical Society)

Mary Peterson
weaving a basket in
Kodiak, May 1991.
(Photograph by the
author)

Mary Peterson playing a stick game with Rena
Peterson, her sister-in-law, 1989. (Photograph by
Rick Knecht, with permission of the Alutiiq Museum
Archives)

Mary's grandsons Dennis and Dwayne Eluska at the Alaska Federation of Natives Convention in Anchorage, 1998. (Photograph by Mike Rostad)

Mary's brother, the late Arthur Peterson, with his wife, Phyllis, and grandchildren Yolanda Inga and Thomas Rastofsoff. (Photograph by Mike Rostad)

Salmon drying against a house in Akhiok, 1985.
(Photograph by the author)

Replica of a traditional *barabara* constructed in Akhiok in 1989 as part of a new cultural program to promote community healing, cohesion, and traditional values. (Photograph by the author)

Mary's son, Mitchell Simeonoff, with kayaks, 1999. (Photograph by Patrick Saltonstall)

Mary Peterson with family members and other villagers at the opening of the traditional *barabara* in Akhiok, 1989. (Photograph by Rick Knecht, with permission of the Alutiiq Museum Archives)

# Exile and Renewal

## Change in Akhiok

"I went through so much, sometimes I wonder if it's true when I think about it, you know, and I can't believe what I went through." These were the first words Mary said to me when we met on a moonlit August night in 1980. I'd had a call at the Kodiak Women's Resource Center that a woman was flying in from Akhiok. The Cessna, packed with villagers coming to town to shop, would carry her away from family problems and the escalating alcoholism in the village. Shadows played over the ghostly forms of the fishing fleet as I drove past the boat harbor to the airport. Mary alighted from the bush plane, a slight figure not quite five feet tall, a silhouette against the blanket of green over Barometer Mountain beyond the airport. Long gray curls cascaded over a thin sweater. Her slightly lined face and still slim figure belied her fifty-three years and eighteen pregnancies. Driving back to town, we shared pleasantries. Mary said little about what had happened. Sadness lingered around her clear eyes. As we rounded Dead Man's Curve toward town, I asked if she was all right, and she repeated the words she'd said earlier, "I can't believe what I went through." The clarity and calm with which she said them triggered questions for me. How had she been able to depart from her life as a daughter, wife, and mother, as a gatherer of berries and plants, a cook, teacher, and basket weaver, a midwife and Community Health Aide?

She left all of that behind because the center of village life seemed to be collapsing. Akhiok had long known hardships, economic and otherwise. In the late twentieth century, a fishing-based economy kept 80 percent of the people employed in summer, but only 12 percent had year-round work. When I arrived on Kodiak in 1979, the average annual income in Akhiok was $6,932. The village store had closed four years earlier. These statistics and facts would not look grim to a traditional elder like Mary, who had lived by subsistence all her life. She had cultural mechanisms for survival. But younger people had grown up with the fallout of economic shifts and accelerated cultural change. With the suppression of the Native language and cultural practices came television and an array of foreign images of how a life should be lived. Slowly, the changes Mary describes gave rise to despair among villagers and to conflicting images of "the good life."[1] Wrenched between worlds of tradition and modernity, between the complex mix of market and subsistence economies, villagers struggled. With money earned through summer fishing and cannery work, the long winter months proved fertile ground for alcohol-related problems to take hold.

All the elders I interviewed told stories about the demonic force of alcohol. Historians speculate that Kodiak's people made homebrew prior to the 1700s, but Russian colonization made alcohol more available. Initially, drinking was a far greater problem among the Russians than it was for Native people, but gradually the manufacture of kvass, a beer made from grain, apples, or roots, became a shared technology.[2] Binges occurred in the nineteenth and early twentieth century, but it was plane service that created deadly, unlimited access in mid-century. In a land of uncertain weather and an unpredictable economy, alcohol became a consistently available and reliable feature of the landscape.

In 1980, Mary was working in the school until noon, then in the clinic until six in the evening. The religious and cultural traditions she clung to as foundations were losing their hold on a younger generation. Escalating alcohol abuse, family violence, the chaos of a village in crisis were all affecting Mary's family and her work. She finally contacted Elaine Loomis at the Kodiak Area Native Association, who called The Kodiak Women's Resource Center.[3] As Mary described her decision to leave, "It was now or never."

In 1985, five years after our initial meeting, I reconnected with Mary. On a visit to the University of Alaska in Fairbanks, I ran into Father Oleksa, a Russian Orthodox priest I'd known on Kodiak. In a casual conversation about my research on Native healers, Oleksa directed me to a Kodiak woman named Mary living in Anchorage who "knows all about traditional healing." A week later, I tracked her to a mustard-colored boarding house near Spenard Road. The door of the clapboard house swung open. There stood the Mary I'd met at the Kodiak airport on the bush flight from Akhiok, the woman who had fled her village and started a new life. She graciously invited me in, but I wasn't sure if she remembered me. What was clear was that Mary Peterson had started over. After her stay at the shelter, she had worked as a volunteer, helping women from other villages, then found a job as a housekeeper.

Mary agreed to talk to me in what would stretch to a decade of interviews. We sat that first day in the Anchorage boardinghouse kitchen, where Mary served tea and smoked salmon. Everywhere were traces of village life: an icon corner, photos of children and grandchildren, sacks of dried herbs and flowers, sheaves of grass for weaving baskets carefully spread on the couch. As Mary spoke, she held a portrait of her son Bobby, an emerging village leader in Akhiok. Distance separated her from him, her other children, even from her own language. She yearned for home.

Yet even in Mary's memory of the "old days," contradictions arose. Nostalgia for the village community merged with the realization that even during her childhood drinking and other problems had already begun to permeate Akhiok. She fought her longing, certain that she could not return to village life.

*Sometimes, when I'm by myself, you know, and I go back, I wish, ooh, I wish them days were here now!*

*I wish it was those days now. Everybody was so nice. They all helped each other and nobody was ever alone. When somebody got married, they'd all get together and get the reception ready. When the men were cutting wood, they would help each other down on the beach. To me, it seemed like it was better because everybody got along. They didn't do much drinking, and if they did, it was just the elderly people and not the young people.*

*The old people, the way they talked about it, they say the Russians started it. They came and traded stuff.*

*One old man used to say that they had foxes all over the village. They'd dry the furs, you know how flat they are, and they'd pile them as tall as a rifle or a shotgun. For those, they'd get the gun.*

*They got gypped so much!*

*If it wasn't for the white people, we'd be better off. They came and changed our way of life. "You'll be better off with that and that," they said. They tried to make money out of us, make us buy and sell. Be-*

*fore, we had our own little houses and got the materials from the cannery. We built 'em real low so in wintertime it wouldn't be cold. When it's too high, all the heat goes up to the ceiling.*

*They brought diseases, all kinds. They say that the white people brought them in, drinking and diseases. Before, people took care of themselves. Sometimes I tell my kids, "I wish it was the old, old days." They never worried about somebody killing himself, somebody drugging himself out, getting drunk, out of control. They just drank to have a good time on a special occasion. Ever since I could remember, everybody was partying in the fall, after they made money. It was not so good for us kids because we had to try to feed the little ones or go to somebody's house that was sober. I grew up and I thought that was the way to live—drink, party all the time.*

*But as I was getting older, I knew that's not the way to live. It was making me sick; I couldn't enjoy anything anymore.*

*Most of them, they weren't violent. And some, they're OK when they're sober, but then they get jealous. My dad got jealous, even when he wasn't drunk, and beat up my mom. But she never left him, and as he grew older, he got better.*

*I was working in the school as a kindergarten teacher in the morning until noon. After that, until six in the evening, I worked in the clinic. Sometimes, I'd be gone all day, and I didn't know what condition I'd find him [her husband] in when I get home. If I didn't drink with him, he'd say I was trying to be an angel, a "goody-goody." He wouldn't leave me alone, even after I had a baby. That's why my kids all catch up with each other [in age]. He'd say, "You're my wife and I can do what I want." My mom and dad tried to talk to him, and he said, "It's my life."*

*Anyway, I don't want to think about that part.*

*In 1980, in August, I left. My kids were all grown, and I had no more responsibilities, just myself, so I had to leave. I was getting to where I was scared all the time. I couldn't stand the drinking anymore. Elaine Loomis from KANA came down to the village and helped me out.*

*I didn't know that she could help! She helped me out of here. I never knew that we could get help from outside the village, but now I know there's help every which way if you ask for it.*

*I didn't want to leave my job, but I had to take care of me. All the stuff that I had started in the village! I hated to leave that, because I love working with the kids and, as a health aide, helping people. But my job is not going to help my health. No matter how much money I have, it won't bring my life back together.*

*There's so much I didn't realize in line of taking care of myself and even IRS papers. I didn't know anything about that until I left. But it feels good to be on your own, you know. If I don't want to cook, I don't have to. I went to Anchorage and people helped me find a job. I worked for elderly people or people that were injured and needed help to care for them. I worked there for two years, then I worked in the schools. I was teaching weaving baskets in the schools. Every month, they have different arts and crafts. When the month came for weaving, I taught it. I think most of them enjoyed it, but it wasn't enough time for me with only six students. I might have to have my own place to teach, or look for another school.*

In the five years Mary had been in Anchorage, she had created a new life, working, teaching, going to church, and visiting with her son Ralph, her daughters Shirley and Vera, and her other children who lived in the city. "I try to help the kids," she said, "cook or clean everywhere I go. Here, the girls won't let me. They'll only let me cook. 'Mom, we miss your cooking,' they say."

Even as she was making a home in Anchorage, Mary gradually began to return to the village for holidays and fishing, feeling her way tentatively toward a possible return. I asked if she was afraid going back to Akhiok.

*Not anymore. The first two years I was. The first year after I left, I didn't go home. Then I started going back home for fishing in the summer because if I don't go fishing, I'm miserable all the time. I make more money there in three weeks or a month than I do in Anchorage all year. Then they kept calling for me at Christmas. You see, I lead the "starring." I had to go because I wanted them to learn. The older girls, they know now. But they still wanted me there, even though they could get by without me.*

*But it's not easy for old people in the village now. It's hard because they don't help people like they used to. I wanted to stay for part of the winter, but I didn't have my own place. And I can't roll a drum of oil. I'd have to hire someone to do it for me. Like, my mom, she has sons and grandsons down there, and she has a hard time. She has to holler before she can get anything done. She has to cut her wood, so I can imagine myself. If I stayed, I'd have the same problem if I didn't have my own place. I could stay with my sons, but even though they might want me to, I feel like I'm intruding. A young couple want to be by themselves without someone listening to them.*

*I went through so much, sometimes I wonder if it's true when I think about it, you know. I can't believe what I went through.*

*But I had good times. I almost went back; I tried to think about the good days. Then I said, "No, I can't!"*

*Kids now, it seems like as soon as the babies start talking, they're sassing the mom. One day, they're going to jump out at the mom and start cussing their parents! If you try to tell them something, they say,*

*"Don't be so old-fashioned!" "It's not old-fashioned," I say. "Old-fashioned people lived better than you do now. They lived well. They behaved well. Kids didn't sass their parents. They didn't beat up their parents. They helped them."*

As we finished speaking, Mary grew silent. I worried that I had posed questions that stirred embers of deep sadness and longing to end her exile. She had opened up to me with raw honesty, generously offering a path into her culture. I felt less like a perpetual outsider, putting a microphone in strangers' faces, taking stories away to analyze. Maybe Mary trusted me because we had a previous link, however brief, when she sought help from the Kodiak Women's Center. But I wasn't sure that she even remembered me. More likely, her generosity to me was another version of the "helping" that had informed her entire life.

## A People in Peril

In 1985, the same year that Mary and I began interviews, I finally made it to Akhiok and glimpsed the circumstances that had driven her from the village. I'd tried to get to Akhiok before, but access is difficult. The southern end of Kodiak still bears marks of the Pleistocene glaciers that erased plant life millennia before. Vegetation is sparse, the winds fierce, and travel conditions unpredictable. Weather can change rapidly. When a clear summer day arrived, I seized the chance. On an average flight, a stranger arriving in a village will be greeted by at least one screeching three-wheeler, children running behind. But when we landed in Akhiok, no one greeted the plane. High winds blew dust over the path; stray dogs roamed between the houses. Arriving in midsummer, I expected to see people out fishing and picking berries, taking advantage of the summer light. But the village seemed deserted. Through the window of one house, I saw five or six men and women around a kitchen table. A tower of beer cans and plates of half-eaten food nearly eclipsed a bingo game in full swing. No one answered when I knocked. I found my way to the clinic, hoping to call for a return plane. I lifted the receiver. Nothing. The phone lines were down. Watching the empty village streets darken, I glimpsed the despair that Mary must have felt when she left.

I finally got a plane out of Akhiok a few days later. Over the next few years, from news and friends' reports, I followed conditions in the village, which continued to disintegrate. In 1987, more than 90 percent of Akhiok's adult population was described as alcoholic.

Then, in January, 1988, a series of articles in the *Anchorage Daily News* linked Akhiok's despair to broader patterns in Native villages throughout Alaska. As I flew into Anchorage that month, my eyes were riveted to the front-page headline, "A Deep Wound, Slow to Heal." "Something is stalking the village people," the article began, "across the state, the Eskimos, Indians and Aleuts of Bush Alaska are dying in astonishing numbers. By suicide, accident and other untimely, violent means, death is stealing the heart of a generation and painting the survivors with despair. A growing sense of helplessness simmers in alcohol throughout the bush. Among a growing percentage of Alaska Natives, life has become equal parts violence, disintegration and despair."[4] For ten days, the paper ran a series of over forty articles, which later received a Pulitzer Prize for journalism. The series, entitled "A People in Peril," chronicled death and cultural destruction throughout Alaskan villages. Always, the articles stressed, alcohol was the final companion of the dead.

At the time that I encountered this article, I had finished graduate school, moved to Seattle, and was en route to Alaska to work with a team of anthropologists on a research project. I also hoped to resume interviews with Mary. Though she still lived in Anchorage, I knew that she would be visiting her daughter Judy in Kodiak when I arrived. We would both be back for a momentous event in Alutiiq history—the first cultural heritage conference ever held on Kodiak. A few weeks later, over a three-day period, anthropologists, historians, and conservation specialists convened to discuss Kodiak's culture. European and Soviet experts captivated crowds herded into the high-school auditorium with accounts of the human remains and art objects taken from the island during the past two centuries. European museums, as well as the Smithsonian Institution, now held more of Kodiak's material culture than the island's Native people. Never before had so many outsiders recognized the legitimacy, the global importance even, of this site where so many cultures crossed.

This outside recognition mirrored new awareness among local people of the rich heritage of Kodiak Alutiiqs. The high-school teacher Dave Kubiak propelled students into oral-history and documentation projects that produced a remarkable local magazine, *Elwani*. Beginning in the early 1980s, Richard H. Jordan directed an archaeological team from Bryn Mawr College that collaborated with local Natives to explore and interpret the prehistory of the island. In addition to Jordan, the archaeologists Rick and Philomena Knecht and then Kodiak Area Native Association Director Gordon Pullar were pivotal figures. They created projects that shared findings with the community and developed opportunities for Native youth to participate. This work eventually stimulated educational outreach programs in the schools, the recording of oral histories, the formation of a traditional dance group, and other activities.[5]

All these changes corresponded with a growing sobriety movement in the villages. Akhiok residents had made dramatic changes over the course of the previous year. In the fall of 1987, government health workers threatened a village couple with the loss of their children if they didn't stop drinking. The couple left the village for an alcohol treatment center in Anchorage. Both said later that they felt a great responsibility; they had been among the heaviest drinkers in the village and had often supplied alcohol to others. After returning to Akhiok, they lived sobriety with messianic zeal. They banned intoxicated people from their home, built a new *banya* and smokehouse, and began an Alcoholics Anonymous group, which met three times a week. Attendance was sparse at first, with only three people coming to the first meeting in December. Then, in January 1988, attendance surged. Returning to Kodiak in February, I found out why.

The same day that the conference ended, I learned about the tragedy in the village of Akhiok that had driven villagers to the AA meeting. The previous month, Mary's son, Bobby Simeonoff, had killed himself after a drinking binge. "Bobby was the one who used to get me firewood," Mary said when I finally found her at her daughter's house in Kodiak. "I knew that I could count on him." We sat on the couch, watching television. She balanced a cup of tea already turned cold. I feared speaking of the death; I feared not speaking of it. She didn't cry as she said, "It's so hard, Joanne."

When Mary could finally talk about Bobby's death, she did so obliquely at first, through the series of losses his death recalled for her.

*My grandpa, he died when I was thirteen. I couldn't quit crying because it seems like that was the first time I experienced death. My little brother, Teacon, was premature. When he died, it was kind* of like—was it true or not? I couldn't get over losing him. Even in school, whenever I thought about him, my tears just came down. Then, a month later, in July, we lost our uncle Davis. I think he had cancer, because he couldn't swallow anymore. So that was a big blow for me. I was kind of his favorite, too, because of his mom's namesake.

*My mom and dad died, two of my sisters, one of my brothers. My sister Marie and I were close. She died, and my brother Senaphant. He slept by me since he was a baby. I don't know what was wrong with him. He coughed all the time, like I did when I was small. I think he had tuberculosis in the blood. They sent him to Unalaska, that was the closest hospital they had. They sent him over there, and he didn't live very long. I think he was only five or six years old. I worried about him so much, you know, like he was my child. I couldn't even go to school. I thought they were lying to us. I told my mom that maybe somebody stole him. They didn't want to send him back because he was cute, like my dad.*

*I guess we'll just have to face what life gives us and try to live with it. In the early days, when children lose somebody in the family, especially one of the parents, the elder person would talk to them so they wouldn't get sick from the loss.*

*The children, losing the small ones wasn't so bad. I know carrying them and losing them was bad, but I wasn't that much attached to them yet, you know. Some of them, a couple of hours or an hour. They're not fully developed yet. But after you live with them for a while and get to know them, when they're there like my son [Bobby], you know, what he did to himself, that was bad. I still feel hurt for him, but what can I do now? Just pray for him.*

*I found out later, I didn't realize that it was getting so bad. He probably did it to himself before he hurt someone else, that's how I*

*feel about it. He was in the council once, and he was the Village Pub-*
*lic Safety Officer, but he quit when he was having a problem. He was*
*having marriage problems, too. I never did find out what went wrong,*
*but what's done is done now. I guess we just have to live with it.*

One striking aspect of Bobby's death was its place in the statewide
pattern illuminated in the *Anchorage Daily News* series. The suicide rate was highest among young men aged twenty to twenty-
four; the national rate in 1988 was 25.6 per 100,000, but for Native men it jumped to 257 per 100,000. Men, the articles asserted,
had become gradually and persistently devalued by Western institutions imposed on traditional cultures. Even the best-intentioned
social programs exacted a price. Though the U.S. government neglected its young territory through the early part of the century,
after World War II government aid expanded. With the growth of
government bureaucracy, many Native women attended school,
found clerical work, or moved to Anchorage. In contrast, the men
began to slide. The economist George Rogers of Juneau summa-
rizes a shift that had begun years earlier: "Suddenly, a male native
was no longer a key person in the survival of his family. A young
mother got welfare payments, older people with Social Security
brought in a tremendous amount of cash. The male was sort of
cast adrift. . . ."[6]

After the death of Mary's son, I wondered if I could ever com-
prehend her life. Was it ethical or even possible to document and
write about her experience? Clearly, the time was not right for
more interviews. I put aside the project, thinking that my work
would be another invasion into the succession of painful incidents in her life. As I left town, I struggled to find a balance between these events: the boost to Alutiiq collective self-esteem

that the conference had engendered and the individual tragedy of Bobby Simeonoff's death. Cultural revitalization might help stay the course of future tragedies. But that knowledge did little to temper the image of Mary's grief, of witnessing another loss in her life.

## The *Exxon Valdez* Oil Spill

In 1991, I wrote to Mary about a return visit. That was a banner year for Kodiak, with national and international attention focused on the island. A Smithsonian exhibit, "Crossroads of Continents," documented the rich cross-fertilization of cultures in the Arctic and Subarctic; many of the artifacts featured came from Kodiak. Local cultural programs continued to thrive as well. The boat builder Joe Kelly supervised the construction of traditional kayaks. The linguist Philomena Knecht created an interactive computer program to teach children the Alutiiq language. In addition, over the course of a decade, the Bryn Mawr College archaeological team had discovered thousands of artifacts. The project, begun near the village of Karluk, expanded to Larsen Bay, Old Harbor, and Kodiak. With each stage, conversations with local communities raised awareness of the riches in the ground. The objects the archaeologists unearthed were housed temporarily in town; calls came for a museum to display and interpret the art and artifacts. Presentations to villagers also kindled new conversations about culture and ethnic identity. Gordon Pullar tells of one woman's reaction to seeing objects such as carved wooden ceremonial masks. "Her facial expression reflected both confusion and sadness. Finally speaking, she said, 'I guess we really are Natives after all. I was always told that we were Russians.'"[7]

Later that year, an event in the village of Larsen Bay put Kodiak on the permanent map of benchmarks in Native American history. On Saturday, October 5, 1991, along the village's single road, a human chain formed to rebury the skulls and bones of 756 Kodiak Natives. In the 1930s, the Czech-born anthropologist Aleš Hrdlička had removed the remains from Larsen Bay to the Smithsonian Institution, where he headed the physical-anthropology division. The reburial ended a five-year struggle with the Smithsonian, marked a milestone in the Native repatriation struggle, and furthered the revitalization of Alutiiq culture. Though some government officials lamented the loss to Western science, others on both sides heralded a new era of more collaborative research and of greater autonomy for Native people. The Bryn Mawr project, in its collaboration with the Kodiak Area Native Association and local people, had already pushed Kodiak in this direction.

That spring, I returned to the north with a research grant from the Alaska Humanities Forum. Mary welcomed me when I met her at her daughter's house in Kodiak, where she was visiting. We decided to talk at the home of my friend Mary Monroe, looking out at the seiners, crab boats, and wooden dories crammed into the boat harbor below. We worked there for the next two weeks, returning to Mary's childhood, her family, and her work as a midwife, material I had recorded before but was happy to hear again. Mary seemed much stronger and even talked about returning to the village. But she was wary, too. The reasons why became clear as I combed the news clips on changes in Akhiok since my visit in 1988.

Tragedy and renewal had continued to punctuate village life. On March 24, 1989, the *Exxon Valdez* rammed a reef in Prince William Sound, dumping 10.8 million gallons of crude oil. Despite the distance, currents carried oil hundreds of miles southwest, affecting nearly one thousand miles of coastal water around Kodiak. The date was Good Friday, a significant marker for Kodiak Natives. On a Good Friday twenty-five years before, many of the same communities were hit by the largest earthquake in North America during modern times. The event had multiple repercussions, negative and positive. Some villages were physically destroyed, which forced residents to relocate, but new skills and technologies also came with community recovery. The earthquake and tsunami that followed remain pivotal in the minds and life stories of Kodiak's Native people, particularly their dual legacy of displacement and adaptability.[8]

The *Exxon Valdez* oil spill didn't hit Kodiak area beaches until mid-April, but the salmon season was ruined for the year, which disrupted the normal cycle of subsistence. In Akhiok, villagers stayed sober through most of the summer as they assisted in the cleanup effort. The men "treated" the oily beaches—the word "cleanup" had been banned by Exxon officials—for the unheard-of wages of $16.69 per hour. Berries went unpicked, fish unharvested, families unattended as Akhiok residents worked round the clock. At first, no one worried when someone cracked a beer after a long day's work. It was not until fall, when Exxon sent out the last of the salary checks, that the most toxic fallout spread. Into the villages, cash flowed with the same rich abundance that the thick oil spread across the seals and ptarmigan and sea life. Like those of an aftershock, the results proved as disastrous.

People in the village began to drink openly. Exhaustive news coverage followed. Tribal Council President Dave Eluska Sr., one of Mary's sons from her first marriage, tried to stress the village's strengths over its frailties. Eluska pointed to the ongoing cultural revitalization as a foundation for recovery. In September, a response team composed of religious leaders, KANA employees, and RuralCap officials, flew to Akhiok to initiate a "healing process." They facilitated "healing circles" to talk about grief, spirituality, and recovery, a melding of the AA model, Russian/Native religious traditions, and cultural revitalization.

The long-term effects of the oil spill would prove most significant. In studies later conducted by anthropologists, Akhiok's reaction was mirrored elsewhere. In interviews with 594 men and women in thirteen communities, researchers found diminished social relations, declines in subsistence practices and in health status, increases in drinking, drug abuse, and domestic violence, and increased post-traumatic stress and depression, especially in women.[9] However, there were also long-term positive effects, including compensatory funding from Exxon. Some funds were directed to publications such as an entire issue of *Arctic Anthropology*, others to building projects, one of which became the Alutiiq Museum and Archaeological Repository.

Further, Nancy Yaw Davis points to community survival strategies that were tested and strengthened by the oil spill. She writes, "The residents in very small communities seem to have a philosophy of tolerance, a resiliency to disruptions, a sense of humor, and a traditional fisherman's perspective that if things are bad this year, they will probably be better next year . . . Also, village residents have family—they are rich in relatives."[10] Another result was a heightened sense of community and unified ethnicity among Alutiiq people. A chief from one village noted that "now we know more about our relatives in Prince William Sound." A series of regional elders' conferences further enhanced this sense of connection. All these shifts would ultimately strengthen the village of Akhiok, but in 1989 the changes that would lead Mary home had not yet fully coalesced.

# Letters: 1991–1992

Mary did get back to Akhiok after Bobby's death and the oil spill, but primarily for visits. She had life-long friends as well as an extensive kinship network in the village: her brothers, Art and Lawrence, her son David and his wife, Luba, and their children, her daughter Laurie Ann and her granddaughter Mary Lynn, and her son Mitch and his wife, Judy. Mary's other children lived in Anchorage, Kodiak, and on the Kenai Peninsula. She journeyed to each place in turn, visiting her growing throng of grandchildren and great-grandchildren. This peripatetic life seemed to suit her, but she always tried to get to Akhiok for holidays.

When Mary went back to Akhiok for Christmas "starring," she sent me a card, a red Hallmark card with a black-and-white bird holding a poinsettia. Inside, she wrote, in careful script:

> Dear Joanne,
>
> I'm doing okay except for a bad cold. Everyone is busy getting ready for starring. For me it is so exciting. I haven't been home this early for a while. I was even here for American Christmas. Get to see the children's Christmas play. I am sitting there watching with a big smile and tears rolling down. Seeing my little grandchildren doing a play and singing so perfect. Gave chills, thrills, tears and what not. I was so glad I made it to town. It reminded me of when we were little—everyone trying to do their best. They were really cute.
>
> God bless you.
>
> With love in Christ, Mary.

These cards became an important source of ongoing connection, a way to keep in touch during the long spells when I didn't see Mary. During the next few years, we began to write letters. I missed the immediacy of our sitting together on rainy Kodiak days, taping her stories, waiting for gusty winds to diminish so Mary could fly back to Anchorage. But I enjoyed being able to picture her at Christmastime in Akhiok, waiting for the mail plane on the long, winding airstrip, winds whipping the tall grass. I imagined her reading the letter by the oil stove, the chill of northeast wind and rain nearly palpable.

In addition to inviting such imagination, literacy confers permanence and greater equality in relationships. During the time that I'd known Mary, the "anthropologist and informant" roles often felt constraining. So many inequities rested on those positions, some of which would never be rectified. But with writing, we were both listeners and tellers, authoring our own worlds, deciding which experiences to share. Our written words enriched how we knew one another.

In February of the following year, Mary sent me a Valentine's Day card from Seward on the Alaska Peninsula. She'd gone for training to resume her job as Community Health Aide in Akhiok. I realized with excitement that she must be going back to live in the village. She wrote, "I am doing fine here for the health aide training . . . but my poor brain hasn't worked this hard since I don't know when. But I am enjoying it, and the best thing is, I am learning something to help someone." Mary was anxious then to get back to the village because her brother Arthur had cancer. She continued, "I haven't been doing too good either (worried, I guess). Sometimes, I can't concentrate (Joanne, what next?) . . . All right, my friend, I shall write again soon." I smiled at the "what next?" I wasn't sure what not doing "too good" really meant. There was much unstated in our relationship. Writing required different modes of translation than oral stories had.

# Return to Akhiok

April 1992. I climbed the grassy knoll behind the Akhiok school as I had on my first visit to the village seven years before. The renewal of spring breathed through the moist tundra, the dwarf birch, the reddish tinge of young willow. Would the changes in people's lives be as palpable as the seasonal shifts? From the bluff where I sat, I imagined the landscape as it was five hundred years before. The silence of the past still reigned here, even though occasionally interrupted by sounds of the present—televisions, boomboxes, CB radios. I leaned into the wind, as though I could feel the centripetal force that drew villagers repeatedly together against the pain of collective demise, the cultural tide that kept this village intact, the pull that brought Mary Peterson back after a decade of exile in Anchorage.

What had finally shifted to allow her reentry? Flying into Alaska, I had read a collection of Tlingit oratory authored by Richard and Nora Dauenhauer, poets from Southeast Alaska dedicated to the conservation of Nora's Tlingit heritage. In the preface, they quote T. S. Eliot's words:

Tradition
Cannot be inherited
And if you want it
You must obtain it
By great labor.[11]

People in Akhiok had labored. Visible from the bluff where I sat, behind a series of wood-frame houses in semicircles, stood a replica of the ancient *barabara*. Villagers had created it the previous year with a grant from the Department of Health and Human

Services. Mary's son, David Eluska Sr., suggested the idea as an alternative to a teen center. The subterranean sod houses in which Native people lived before Europeans arrived rose as symbol of the traditional spirit now invoked to combat alcoholism and other problems. After the *Exxon Valdez* oil spill, the village stabilized, then backslid; possible relapse threatened every rebirth of sobriety. Western mental-health models proved as impotent to battle behavioral illness as shamans once had been against smallpox and other infectious diseases. But a new cultural narrative had opened, and the tool for healing village life was proclaimed to be tradition. The *barabara*, new language programs, the building of kayaks—each aspect of this cultural flowering helped open the way for Mary's return.

I hadn't let myself believe that Mary was really back. In her letter from Seward, she had written: "I'm here to learn new things health-wise, but I am anxious to get home." Home. I had never heard her call Anchorage or Kodiak "home." After all these years, I would actually meet Mary in the landscape she had described with deep longing, as though her feet might never touch this soil again. Mary knew that I might be coming; the time was indefinite because of weather conditions. I hoped to surprise her with my arrival for Easter.

I found Mary in a small house near the clinic at the far end of the village. "I wondered if that could be you!" She held open the door, and gave me a hug. As she finished preparing her *kulich* (Easter bread), Mary described the changes in the village and how it felt to be back. She repeated some of the stories she'd told me the previous spring. She spoke of her son Bobby and how his suicide had spurred villagers to action. In particular, Mary stressed how healing was served by renewal of "the old ways"—holiday traditions, language, the beliefs and practices of "being Aleut," including her traditional basketry.

*They [the villagers] just did it themselves, which I'm really proud of. After he [Bobby] died, they were telling each other what alcohol was doing, and there were several attempts after that. My nephew and someone else, and even the women—Ahh! They're afraid what might happen to their kids if they kept drinking, you know, and that kind of woke them up. They all try to help each other now with AA meetings. They had to find a way to get people to come to the meetings; they'd tell them, "It's not to stop you from drinking, it's just explaining what alcohol does to people." They got more and more people, especially the men.*

*Then, first thing you know, the women have their own healing get-together. It gets them to see each other and talk about how they used to do things and how good they feel to be doing something instead of craving for alcohol. Some of them take a drink once in a while, but they don't bother the others. They just stay home so the kids won't see them. They don't want their children to grow up in that environment, so if they stay sober, the kids will. How good it feels for us to stay sober!*

*It really amazed me. Last year, when I went home for Christmas, I was so amazed and surprised. No drinking with the starring, you know. I was just surprised and I even felt like crying.*

*It started before. One winter in '87 when I didn't go, I went to Chignik, and then I heard the tapes [of Christmas songs from Akhiok] in the spring. They sounded so good. I just wanted to throw out the ones I made before. Ooh! They sounded like a bunch of alcoholics before. I had to separate that tape so that nobody would hear it. I was one of them and I felt ashamed of it, listening to the new tape. They*

*sounded so nice, clear, and good. Then when I went the next years in*
*'89 and '90, it felt so good not to see everybody stumbling around and*
*messing up the caroling. Everybody stayed right with us, even the*
*children, with their little plastic bags, collecting candy.*

*Now it's good because they're sober and the tapes are better. I'd tell*
*them, you know, "Try to record it so that it won't get lost. You keep*
*doing it as you grow older and then teach your kid's kids and let it*
*live." New Year's and Russian Christmas. It was kind of fun when*
*they're willing to still do those things so they could remember and tell*
*their kids. They go starring, but not the Devil's Dance. They don't do*
*that anymore. They just go from house to house, shake hands with*
*the New Year, try to get that Old Year out. That's all they do in homes*
*where there's little children that might get scared. Then they're hol-*
*lering "Happy New Year!" Everybody's dancing, having a good time.*
*In Kodiak, they have a* Praznik *[celebration] at the Elks. It's just mas-*
*querading, and they win prizes and dance. They have accordions and*
*guitars and Russian dancers. They'll have maybe a couple hours for*
*the older people, the old-time music, then, later on, rock music.*

*That's why they're doing this, to keep it going. I think when KANA*
*first started, they tried to pick up the old traditions. They want to*
*keep them going so they won't die away and get lost, especially the*
*language.*

Mary brought out a pile of drying grass from the closet, a sight
familiar to me from our very first interview in Anchorage. Even
while away from the village, she gathered grass and wove baskets.
Mary practices an open weave of basketmaking sometimes called
"Old Harbor" style. Kodiak weavers also produce a more tightly
woven, detailed basketry called *Attu* that spread to Kodiak from
the Aleutian Islands.[12]

I tell my kids, "Don't let it get lost!" This we don't want to lose. We've lost so much—arts and crafts, things our people used to do and never taught us how to do, like skin sewing, making raincoats from bear guts.

The baskets—I think I had three children when I first did one. I just was around this old lady from Old Harbor, Fedosia Inga her name was. She used to come to Alitak in the summer to work. She'd pick grass early in the morning and I'd go with her. I just liked being with her. She'd be telling me stories, she'd laugh so much! I just watched her and finally I told her, "I'm gonna try." It didn't take me long because whenever we weren't working, we were together. My sisters were busy watching the kids, and I was with her most of the time.

You have to pick grass from along the beach, you know. Big, wide blades of grass. The best time is in September because they're longer and they're green. You have to get them before it starts raining, then they get black spots on them. If they're long enough, you can weave them soon after you pick them. She [Fedosia Inga] would just sit there on the beach and start weaving. If they're too dry, then you have to soak them to let them get soft or they just crack. Even if they're short, pick them for the spokes. Every fall, I pick a bunch or two. I think to myself, "Well, if I happen to get by myself someday, I'll have something to do."

I put a bottle in them sometimes to shape it. Let it get real nice and round and put weight on it so that the bottom will flatten out. Then the lining, you know, put that inside with some kind of cloth.

I give them to my kids. There was one lady, she bought one for five dollars. When I think about it, I think, "Oohh, I lost out on that one." We talked to Eunice Neseth. She said, "They're worth more than that because they're fine work." Hers are real fine, that Attu way. The grass is split and split again.[13]

*We don't want it to get lost. My grandma made baskets at one time. They used them for berries and for bread. I remember my grandma would put a towel inside and put biscuits in it. You'd use them to hold anything—beads, buttons. They say that a long time ago they used them for hauling water. They put sealskin inside, I think, or seal stomach. They'd dry it, blow it up, then use it for seal oil. As my grandma grew older, she couldn't make them anymore. She never sewed, like those raincoats made out of bear guts. Her eyes were getting bad so that by the time I grew to know her she wasn't doing it.*

*I taught my daughters how, and some of the kids in Akhiok. They got the idea, and, like me, they'll pick it back up again.*

Mary gave me a *kulich* to bring back to Kodiak. Bread under my arm, I meandered through the village. Children played again on the dusty paths near the community center, where several villagers scrubbed the room for the next day's Easter potluck. Soon the tables would be laden with duck, smoked salmon, turkey, jello salads and Tang, *kulich*, and *perok*, the traditional salmon-and-rice pie.

I walked back to the school, where I was staying. I had waited to attend this central Russian Orthodox holiday for over a decade, since I first saw a photograph of the Akhiok church. At 11:30 P.M., I found my way to the women's side, several rows behind Mary, as the reader began to sing in Church Slavonic. Hanging icons, pink and yellow paper flowers prepared by village women weeks ago, and rows of elaborately frosted *kulich* filled the church with color. The villagers' chants rose into the dome of the church. A child in a faded ski jacket held her candle to mine, sharing the flame. We carried our flickering lights outside to circle the church three times, the initiation of the ceremony. Mary walked ahead of me, radiant in the candle light. She was home.

The day after the big Easter celebration, I found Mary at work in the clinic. I asked how the holiday seemed compared to the days she remembered so well and had longed for in Anchorage. She expressed pleasure at the continuity, but also longing for a quality of life now gone, a kind of "homesickness" even when home.

*The Slavonic songs made Easter feel like the old ways. Mostly, it's in English now, but they're still doing it the same way, like they always did. Those of us that know, we're trying to make sure the younger kids know what to do when we're not around. I told one of the boys to try to remember what they see in church so they'll know about what to do for Holy Thursday and Good Friday, how to handle the icons. Like me, when I was young, they told us these things. They left me for a while, but now they've come back to my mind. I remember somebody telling me these things, and I put them together, picturing what they did, and I helped them on Good Friday.*

*It feels so good to be home. I haven't been home in the early spring for so many years. It brings back memories from the time we were growing up. I just close my eyes and I go back to when I'm nine, ten, eleven years old. I can see people getting ready for the Easter holiday.*

*But even when I'm home, I still feel homesick because of how people used to get ready for Easter and everything in the spring. I miss how they lived. Everybody helped each other. They all went after wood, helped each other. To me, it felt so comfortable. Everybody was just looking forward to Easter. It felt like you were looking forward to something big because everybody fasted; then it was a big party when we got to eat what we hadn't eaten during Lent. It feels good for somebody that really feels it! I don't how to express it. It just makes you feel good to know everybody's getting ready for the holiday.*

*Afterward everyone was so quiet, fulfilled with something they were waiting for. I know I miss that. But still, we did that in Anchorage, the families up there. We all invited each other for food and tried to respect the land, even though we're not home, those of us that are from the villages.*

In the white-walled clinic, we sat surrounded by cupboards of medicine, bandages, and syringes. I asked how it felt to be back as the Community Health Aide in the context of the villagers' sobriety.

*It's much, much better now! It [reform] had started before I left, with very few, you know. But now there's more. It's calmer now. When a few people do party, it's not as wild as it used to be. It's much better. I remember when I was a health aide here, I couldn't relax when they were drinking. I had to be awake, and I'd get scared when they pounded on the door. They never just knocked! They expected me to get up and get dressed. It's not like that anymore. They respect our hours now. If they get sick and it's not very serious, then they wait until the next day. They're not demanding like they were when I first started. It's getting much better.*

*It feels good to be doing something for somebody. If I wasn't working here, I don't know what I'd be doing. Helping people in their homes. I still do whatever people need. Especially now. If they need help, I go.*

*But I don't know what I'll do. If I stay here, I'll have to pay so much for a house, plus oil and lights. We have to have oil and wood. I just can't tell anybody to go and get me wood. Even my kids. Even though they would, I feel that I need somebody who would do it, anyway. I just don't like to tell people what to do. I don't like to ask because I'm afraid I'll get turned down. Or I'm afraid they'll say, "I'm* busy." So I just don't ask. Things I can do I'd rather do myself. If I ask, I know they would.

My kids don't want to believe I'm old! [Mary would be sixty-five the following year.] "No, Mom, you're not that old yet." They see me working around, doing things, traveling around, house cleaning, walking, working, and fishing. "No, you're not old yet." I told my son Ralph, "I think I'll quit working and sell my [fishing] permit and just stay home." He said, "No, Mom, if you quit working you'll get old. You'll sit around and waste yourself. You just keep working as long as you can." I say, "Well, gee, I have to quit sometime."

If I didn't need to make money, I'd go visiting all over! My friends and my kids.

## A Gathering of Midwives

January 1993. Mary and I unpacked our bags in adjacent rooms in a hotel near Turnagain Arm in Anchorage. With new concert halls, wine bars, and multiplex theaters, the city had changed a great deal since the rough-and-tumble oil pipeline era of the 1970s. We'd arrived on a clear, brisk night for a gathering of traditional midwives to begin the next day. The event was sponsored by the Alaska Maternal Child Health Coalition and by Chugachmiut, the organization that serves Native people of the lower Kenai Peninsula and Prince William Sound region. Many of the medical personnel who attended the conference, Native and non-Native, were trained in Western medicine. In addition to nurses and doctors, there were young women seeking information about home births, and village people who wanted to learn more about their cultures. The midwife, conduit of biological continuity, had become a symbol of cultural connection as well.

The gathering focused on the midwives' stories, narratives driven underground for many years, now eagerly sought by an audience excited about the possibilities of traditional healing. Peppered with phrases about "knowing" and "believing" in the midwife, these stories had been told not in history texts or popular accounts but among and between women. Though written histories labeled the midwives' work officially "dead" with the gradual movement toward hospital deliveries, the oral tradition circulated with a quiet, but fierce, determination to survive. If, as Harold Napoleon asserts, the loss of the traditional healer's efficacy spelled the demise of Native cultures, this focus on her power symbolized cultural renewal.

Mary and I shared a cab to the gathering in the morning. I'd picked her up from her daughter's house, where numerous grandchildren hung on her arms, pleading with her to stay. When we arrived, the public radio station was setting up to record. Other midwives had come from the Kenai Peninsula and throughout Southwest Alaska to form a lively and informative panel. Many were both midwives and Community Health Aides (CHAs), illustrating the historical connection. In addition to Mary there were Elenore McMullen, the Chief of Port Graham, a licensed practical nurse, and a CHA; Matuska (Mother) Platonida Gromoff, the wife of a Russian Orthodox priest, who had practiced midwifery as a CHA in Unalaska and on Kodiak; Feona Sawden, a CHA from Port Graham and an expert in the use of native plants in healing; and Margaret Eskilida, a midwife who had delivered most of the adults in her village of Chitina near Copper River, northeast of Anchorage.

Laughter often filled the room, as when Feona Sawden told of how to differentiate cockles from other clams (the clams look like females, the cockles like males, Feona claimed, declaring, "We eat the males!"). Or when Platonida Gromoff revealed how long she had believed she would get pregnant if a man touched her. The audience of Native and non-Native health-care practitioners listened attentively, captivated by descriptions of medicinal plants, dietary restrictions, prenatal treatment in the *banyas*, and postpartum caring for the mother. Ninety-one-year-old Margaret Eskilida described her puberty seclusion of nearly a year with a veil over her face; she detailed how women used to pull on a rope suspended from the ceiling as they delivered. Silence ruled when Elenore McMullen told of how her grandmother would deliver babies in hunting and fish camps, lining a pit with moss. She also described the pain and loss both mother and midwife sometimes faced. "The woman's husband would be gone for days," McMullen said, "and the baby might be buried before he returned."

A tremendous outpouring of knowledge about healing emerged that day, saved beyond the immediate performance by tape and video recorders. Mary was particularly impressive telling about her practices as a midwife. I'd only heard her stories in private; now, in performance, she shone. Some beliefs the other women described echoed those I'd heard from Mary, such as the admonition against crocheting or standing in a doorway during pregnancy to avoid having the cord wrapped around the baby's neck. Matuska Gromov told a "midwife to the rescue" narrative I'd heard from a number of women on Kodiak. In this version, Matuska offers to aid a non-Native nurse living in her village. The woman declines, claiming she is teaching her husband all he needs to know to act as midwife. They even make a bed with stirrups to simulate the hospital scene. But in the final hour, at 2:30 A.M., the husband comes screaming for help, and the midwife arrives in the nick of time. The story elicited peals of laughter and confirmed the collective belief in the power of midwifery and traditional knowledge.

Mary also told stories that were new to me; often, they were prompted by other women's remembrances. This interplay of stories showed how important context is for eliciting narratives. While this gathering was not a traditional setting for storytelling, it revealed the need for new arenas for sharing such stories with diverse audiences.[14] With public-radio personnel and video cameras situated throughout the room, the conference also illustrated what Walter Ong calls "secondary orality," the telling of stories via electronic media that links oral cultures to their past and extends the community of listeners.[15] Some of the conference proceedings would also find their way into print, furthering the life of this knowledge. Both the written and electronic record connect these traditional healers to the growing alternative health community and help establish the legitimacy of parallel systems of knowledge.

Elenore McMullen opened the discussion by detailing her thirty-four years in health care as a licensed practical nurse, as a Community Health Aide, and as a "young girl helping my grandmother." She described how she became a midwife by going around with her grandmother as her "runner." Elenore prompted Mary's recall of her own apprenticeship, illustrating the importance of context for the performance of stories and the collective shaping of narrative.

*Like her, I was working with the other midwives. But at first, they wouldn't let me into where the baby was being born. But I stayed right there, ready. Then they'd holler, "Go get this, do that." Later on, when my mom was alone, then she started letting me help her. I just watched her. I kind of learned by myself, too, just watching. She didn't really have the patience to teach, but she'd tell me, "Just watch what I do." And I learned by myself when I had my babies.*

*There's so many things that we could use and we could sterilize ourselves. We don't have to buy everything. For the bellybutton, they used a quarter or a fifty-cent piece to put on the bellybutton and hold it in. They kept that binder around the baby so it looked like a mummy; I never saw how they changed it. After everyone was finished walking in and out, that's the only time they changed the baby so it wouldn't get cold. And they always had little houses where the mothers were so that the baby wouldn't get cold. When I see them on TV or in the hospital, I think "Oh, that baby's cold!" There's nothing but air and hardly any covers.*

*They never gave babies a bath; they're afraid they might get cold, but they wiped their faces once in a while. They used that Wesson oil on the baby and cleaned them up—that same oil they used to light the candles and the icon. After the baby's born, I could smell that oil smell all the time.*

Prompted by Margaret Eskilida's story of how women in her village used hair to sew up wounds, Mary recalled the use of sinew in traditional healing on Kodiak.

*I heard that, too. If a woman has a baby, anything that was nearby, they'd tear it and use the end of their dress or their hair, the midwives. My mom told me they always carried sinew, dried sinew, in their pocket all the time, and a little scissors and cloth to bind the bellybutton. I always wondered why she'd be chewing gum all the time. It wasn't gum, it was sinew. She was making it soft. It's real stiff, that bear sinew. They used it for thread before and made raincoats out of bear gut and seal gut. Midwives had that bag filled with sinew and a whole big roll of cloth that looked like Ace bandages, only it was flannel. A big roll of it. After the baby's born, after they first poop, then they wrapped the poor baby up and made it look like a mummy. They always had a little bag with all those things in it. When my mom was a midwife, there weren't as many pregnancies like before. There used to be eight to ten pregnancies at once, and the midwife had to be ready all the time.*

Feona Sawden told of how the midwives used a ball of flannel under a woman to speed the delivery. This story followed Elenore McMullen's description of how her grandmother placed several folds of flannel under a woman's rectum to minimize tearing and speed delivery: "In my grandmother's bag was a piece of flannel. During the time when the baby was coming, my grandmother would fold that up several thicknesses and put it on the mother's rectum so that she wouldn't have hemorrhoids. I thought it was such a wonderful, beautiful thing. It minimized the tear, too." Mary followed with her own recollection: "Sometimes, we'd wrap the towel even, for her comfort, or let her move it to where it will hit her at the right place. While she's in labor, she's sitting on that. It really helps."

Each of Feona's and Elenore's descriptions elicited similar ones by Mary, beginning and ending with stories of how quickly the deliveries used to go. The cycle of remembrance wove together like a thick braid.

*We used the banya to relax the woman's muscles, especially at eight to nine months, and hot-packed them in the bath so they won't labor very long. If you're tense all the time, everything starts hurting. If they have back pain, then we used to use a green fern to make a lin-*

iment to rub on them. They never laid mothers down when they delivered; the mothers crouched down. It was faster.

For the placenta, if it wouldn't come out right away, we put a safety pin in seal oil that has been aged a little. Drink a tablespoon of that to help the placenta come out. The placenta was sacred; it was something like a sacred thing. They never just took it and threw it [out]. They cleaned it and checked to see if any pieces were broken out. They didn't touch it with their hands; they used a stick to move it around. Then they wrapped it up in a clean cloth and put it in a small box or a can and buried it away from the village behind a hill. The husbands took it and buried it so that the next time they get pregnant, they wouldn't have problems. They say that if you don't treat the afterbirth like a human, you'll have problems. They say the afterbirth is very jealous. If it's not treated like a human, the next one might be problems. They treat it like a human. There was one old lady, who was blind, who would say, "Why not treat it like a human? That's what's making the baby live in your stomach." That's almost the most important thing. They really, really respected it.

They never used to take long to deliver. The last two months, the midwives take them for walks every day. The midwives always carried their little bag; they always had big pockets to carry whatever they need in case the mother had the baby in the road somewhere. Plus their little snuffbox. They ground up the snuff until it was powdery. If the mother labors too long, then the midwife would put a little bit in her nose to try to make her sneeze and help the labor. Sure enough, the water would break and the labor would go faster. So many things that I've seen and heard!

A question-and-answer session followed the midwives' discussion. Mary sat with hands folded in her lap, waiting for questions.

A young blond woman who'd identified herself as a nurse asked how Mary had been compensated for her work. Mary hesitated, as though she hadn't understood the question. The young woman tried again. "What did you get from the people in the village?" Mary was silent at first, then she responded, simply, "This is God's work." Left with the sense that not everything could be explained, we dispersed for the day.

Mary and I made plans to have dinner that night. At the hotel, I drifted off to sleep, lulled by the drone of a television down the hall. When I awakened, our appointed meeting time had passed. The phone in Mary's room rang, an empty echo. I hurried to the front desk to find a note on Westmark Hotel stationery.

> My dear Joanne M., See you again, Sometime, again — God bless you — Went to see my son, Ralph. Take care and be careful. Good luck, Mary

Sadness filled me, coupled with fear that we wouldn't meet again. If she'd told me orally, perhaps I wouldn't have felt the same way. Perhaps it's simply writing, its sense of rigid closure. As Walter Ong points out, the "startling paradox inherent in writing" is its association with death, recalling the Platonic charge that "writing is "inhuman, thinglike" and that it "destroys memory." [16] Contradictions and ironies abounded. The conference illustrated the power gained by Native people through sharing their stories via the "secondary orality" of electronic media and via literacy. In my relationship with Mary, letters had opened up new worlds, but now written words, even if full of affection, seemed severe in their finality. They stood in stark contrast to the fullness of the stories that had filled the conference room earlier. I wondered when I would see Mary again.

# Letters: 1993–1995

Even when I didn't get back to Kodiak for years, Mary continued to write, keeping me abreast of changes in her life and in the village. The year the midwifery conference took place, Mary sent a three-page Christmas missive, written on both sides. She was in her own home in Akhiok now, up at 5 A.M., decorating the house for Christmas. She had quit her job as a health aide, grateful to have time alone to sew and weave.

Mary described the climate changes in detail: "Our weather here is just unpredictable. We had snow on the mountains the first week of September. Very little. Then our first blanket of snow on Thanksgiving. Then it rained and was gone, then the wind blew. Right now we have westerly winds 20 to 30 and cool, cool, then warm, cold, rain, snow, then windy and calm." I remembered how hard the winds blew across the open expanse of Akhiok, how a local Native meteorology had emerged through centuries of watching the landscape and surrounding waters. Mary continued, "It sure feels good to be by myself and on my own and do whatever I want to do, like writing a letter in the wee hours of the day. Eat and sleep and clean up whenever I feel like it. When I'm by myself, I can leave my handwork on my table until I pick it up again with no disturbance. I'm telling you, Joanne, it sure feels good! I weave once in a while, knit, crochet, and sew. I'm working on a quilt right now, but my problem is in trying to piece them together. I guess what I should do is close my eyes, grab a piece and sew it together. Since I got my own place, I don't go anywhere. Just stay at home and try to amuse myself with my handwork, and read, read, read—ahh! and watch soaps whenever."

I had sent Mary several short essays I'd written that drew on our work together. One focused on Mary's life, another was a memoir of my experiences in Alaska.[17] I sought her comments before they were published. Had I interpreted her words as she meant them? Should I use her real name and that of the village? Repercussions can follow from publishing about a place, but I felt that Mary's strength and the resilience of Kodiak's Native culture deserved attention as real people and events.

About the articles I'd sent, Mary joked, "My daughter Laurie Ann picked up my mail and said you got a package from your friend. 'Oh, yeah?' I said. Then I saw the mail and said, 'Oh, no—that's a bunch of reading material!'" Her reaction so contrasted with her pleasure in reading magazines and other publications that I wondered: Did she mean it? Was this documentation of her life really a burden she had politely endured? She wrote little about the article concerning her life, saying only that she had passed it on to her children. I thought that a good sign. But I still couldn't interpret exactly what she meant. With writing, a permanent record exists, but permanence may not ease the confusion or difficulty of communicating across cultures.

Mary's letters described her visits to Kodiak and Anchorage, most recently for the Alaska Federation of Natives (AFN) annual gathering. She also detailed some of the problems she'd encountered upon moving back to the village, particularly making ends meet financially. Her Social Security payments had been temporarily suspended, and the office in Juneau couldn't find her birth certificate. "I guess I don't exist," she joked. "But I'm doing OK anyway. Good thing I have three sons here. They help me a lot." Even as she expressed gratitude for family in the village, Mary also wrote with longing for the past when financial help was less necessary, when "everyone was one big family." As she often had in oral narrative, she lamented the passing of a way of life before market exchange. "Nowadays, we have to have money to have anyone do anything for you. Before, everyone helped one another. When anyone got sick, ran out of food or clothes, the second chief, what we call now the 'vice-president' would go collect from people."

Mary's letter also expressed contradictory feelings about transformations in village life. Some of those changes had motivated her resignation as the CHA. Whereas in the "old days" everyone "helped one another," the CHA now fulfilled the helping role to a stressful degree. The demands to do "every little thing" and be available beyond working hours were simply too taxing. On the other hand, change and modernized health care, which complemented the CHA's work, now brought a doctor to the village monthly. This had enabled Mary's daughter Laurie Ann to return to Akhiok. She required medical assistance because of a heart condition, and the doctor's monthly visit provided her with the shots necessary to avoid infection.

The integration of traditional and Western life leaves many such contradictions intact, affecting not only medicine, education, local governance, and employment, but also the attitudes of people toward those realms. In Mary's letter, she expressed dismay at the lack of well-funded jobs for village people, even as she continued to yearn for the days when market considerations had little importance in village economies.

Mary ended that letter, which she'd started at 5 A.M., with, "Okay, you take care now. I thought of you and my children on Thanksgiving. It was first time in a long time that I cooked dinner. My sons said, 'We finally got some of Mom's Thanksgiving dinner.' My house is small but we managed. I could go on and on, but it's 7:55 and I'm getting hungry. Boy, it looks like I wrote a book here!"

The following summer, Mary sent a card with a sobering message. On its pink-and-gray cover a bunch of roses framed the words: "The Rose Still Grows beyond the Wall." The message inside read:

Shall claim of death
cause us to grieve
and make our courage faint or fall?
Nay, let us faith and hope receive
The rose still grows beyond the wall.

I thought of her son Bobby's death and of all the losses she'd sustained. Despite the packaged sentiment of the card, the message about faith and hope seemed apt, as they remained the constants in Mary's life.

The letter, in contrast to the sober tone of the card, was joyful. "I'm so glad your berries are getting ripe. Ours are only now blooming. Salmonberries, lowbush Alaskan cranberries, and what they call crowberries." She announced a veritable heat wave of sixty-two degrees. I remembered well how people in Kodiak wilted on such a day, closing things down to go fishing. She added, in reference to my ongoing attempts to edit her life history: "And about the book. I hope it will be out soon. I'm anxious to read it. Good luck with your studies and summer school. When I don't hear from you, well, Ah, you know . . . My kids don't write because they call me on the phone. The only good mail I get is from you. Everything else is junk mail and bills." She thanked me again for the *Family Circle* magazine I gave her each year for Christmas. She was trying recipes and reporting back to me. I often sent Mary tea and scented soaps, things hard to get in the village. This time, with characteristic tact, she wrote, "I sure enjoy the soaps. If you decide to send tea and soap, please put the tea in a zip lock bag so it won't taste like soap."

I wrote back, sending a bar of lavender soap. The English breakfast tea flew off in a separate package.

## Ways of Knowing

I did not see Mary again until 1996, when I returned to Kodiak for a conference sponsored by the Alaska Rural Systemic Initiative. This project, based at the University of Alaska Fairbanks, sought to integrate elders' traditional knowledge into Western educational curricula and institutions. An influential book helped spawn the effort: *A Yupiaq World View: A Pathway to Ecology and Spirit* by Angayuqaq Oscar Kawagley.[18] The author illustrates the different paths and strengths of Western and Native worldviews and discusses how they might best be combined. The project coordinators brought elders from Kodiak villages together to share knowledge of weather, environmental patterns, healing, and other forms of Native science.

Outside attention to Alutiiq culture augmented the increasing sense of pride among local people. Through the early 1990s, innovative cultural programs in town and in the villages continued the revitalization process begun a decade earlier. Exemplary is the increasingly popular "Dig Afognak," a project that brings outsiders to the island to work with archaeologists and local Natives in collecting and preserving local artifacts. Other projects have built Native sod houses (*barabaras*, or *ciqlluaqs*), kayaks (*baidarkas*, or *qayaqs*), painted hunting hats, and revived and taught songs and dance traditions.

How far Alutiiq people had come is illustrated by a look back at one of the first elders' gathering in the 1980s. Roy Madsen, a

Kodiak Native, had related a tale called "Atliuvatu's Song," the story of a weak, sickly elder who reminisces about his youth, when people were healthy. Madsen ended with a request for the young people to listen to their elders who "lived in harmony with the land . . . so that they can be proud once more. Help us to remember and be strong again." The parallels to contemporary Native culture were obvious, as was the plea to the youth present to pay attention to the few remaining elders who spoke Alutiiq and who remembered the lost villages, the songs and dances—those who embodied the culture's "healthy state."

Ten years later, Alutiiq culture was pink-cheeked with good health. Perhaps the most visible and enduring sign was the opening of the Alutiiq Museum and Archaeological Repository in May 1995. Commenting on the symbolic integration of Russian and Native cultures, the local paper, the *Kodiak Daily Mirror*, noted that "it is no accident that the 18,000 square-foot turquoise and white building blends well with its neighbor's blue onion dome and white clapboard siding." The museum's collection includes contributions of objects from local people as well as artifacts returned from museums, colleges, and national and international collections. Natives of Kodiak and the Kodiak Area Native Association developed the project, aided by a $1.5 million grant from the *Exxon Valdez* Oil Spill Trustee Council. Returning to Kodiak a year after the museum opened, I was stunned by how central a place this building—and the culture it represented—now held in a community that two decades earlier had declared its demise.

When I arrived in September, scattered stands of deciduous trees bronzed the landscape. I found the conference underway in the new KANA building, where elders faced one another across an oblong table, discussing ways to predict weather patterns. Native elders, KANA employees, and a professional taping crew, now a ubiquitous feature at Native gatherings, packed the conference room. Elders from various villages described knowledge of the waters and discussed navigational decision making and their frustration at licensing exams that tested knowledge of waterways in New England. Mary's expertise in native plants, traditional healing, and other areas made an essential contribution to the discussion. Though she had long been an important presence in the village, she now clearly held the acknowledged status of elder.

That afternoon, Mary had to leave suddenly, complaining of severe pains. Someone returned later to announce that she had been hospitalized. I pondered the vast network of Alaskans who would feel panic at this news. So many people loved and relied on her, an ever widening circle of kin—sixty-five grandchildren and great-grandchildren at last count. I visited the hospital each day, waiting my turn when the line of visitors grew lengthy. We talked again about the book; questions remained; I meant to interview her to fill in gaps. But each time I thought about taking out the tape recorder, I stopped. Her vulnerability in a hospital bed made "collecting" seem rapacious and inappropriate. When I left Kodiak, she had nearly recovered from digestive problems and was ready to return to the village. But she would wait for the weather to break, anticipating just the right time. "I always know when I'm ready, when it feels right. I just follow my feeling, whatever it is. Same way with telling my kids things. When my insides feel like it, when something says, 'Now, now, tell them now,' that's when I do."

## We Are One

As early as 1991, the Native scholar Gordon Pullar and others began to call for a reconvening of Alutiiq people now dispersed

throughout sixteen villages on Kodiak Island, the Alaska and Kenai Peninsulas, and the Prince William Sound region. Through
the twentieth century, a number of events had contributed to
breaking ties between Alutiiq villages: the Katmai eruption of
1912, the 1964 Good Friday earthquake, an influx of non-Natives
into the fishing industry, and, most significantly, the creation
of separate village and regional corporations with the passage of
the Alaska Native Claims Settlement Act in 1971.[19] Political
movements and events following the *Exxon Valdez* oil spill had
prompted increased unity among Alutiiqs; still, a lack of cohesion
persisted. In proposing a regional gathering, Pullar had called for
an event to "reunite the communities . . . thereby promoting community, family, and individual healing" and to offer a place "to discuss alternatives for cultural revitalization and community healing, development, and growth."[20] Such a gathering, people hoped,
would renew old ties, rekindle kinship connections, and foster
broad cultural and political unity.

Thus it was with tremendous enthusiasm that the first regional
Alutiiq Elders' Conference opened in 1997. The conference illuminated the complex nature of Native identities at the end of the
twentieth century: local, regional, national, and global. A revered
elder, Larry Matfay, opened the conference by lighting a traditional oil lamp, its stone base laid over strands of beach grass, a
long wick of light blazing through a bath of seal oil. The hearty
guide who had led bear hunters through Kodiak's dense interior
for years now seemed frail in a thin blue parka, but Larry's spirit
remained strong. The Alutiiq Dancers sang and drummed. Their
fur-trimmed red, white, and black outfits, replicas of the traditional "snow falling" parkas, connected them to their ancestors.
The original garments were constructed from the shiny throat

skins of cormorants, trimmed with tassels of red leather, white fur, and puffin beaks, which floated as the dancers moved, simulating falling snow.[21] Other dancers wore replicas of traditional hunting hats with long pointed beaks, painted brilliant blues and reds. The long black robes of Father John Zabinko and other Russian Orthodox priests contrasted with the dancers' bright garb.

Excitement suffused the three days of workshops and sessions convened for the purpose of assessing artifacts, archival records, and photographs. Cultural issues that had been neglected or driven underground stimulated open discussion. Rena Peterson (formerly Cohen) of Akhiok spoke at length about learning to heal from Oleanna Ashouwak. Stories long told in private were now openly shared, narrated with pride rather than fear as to how they might be interpreted. Before the end of the weekend, participants called for an ongoing effort to reconnect these long-divided communities.

I missed the 1997 gathering, but I gleaned the energy and momentum it generated through watching the videos and hearing reports. In 1998, I was determined to make it for the second elders/youth conference. The opening ceremony echoed that of the previous year, as did its theme: "Allriluukut—We are One." The brightly dressed dancers stood alongside Father John, but this year Elder Lucille Davis, dressed in ceremonial regalia, rose to light the lamp. Florence Pestrikoff followed, with a stirring tribute to her deceased father, Larry Matfay. The loss of two respected elders, Larry Matfay and Ignatius Kosbruk, had darkened the previous year. But their legacy, like the long wick stretched through seal oil, had been ignited the year before and now burned with a low, insistent intensity.

At the conference, Western and Native cultures blended, regional ties renewed, and discussion ranged from national politics to global issues. The complex decisions contemporary Native people face were temporarily suspended on Saturday night. Accordion and guitar players brought elderly couples to the hotel dance floor to waltz, polka, and swing until late in the evening. The dance culminated in the celebration of Mary's seventy-first birthday.

Mary's presence at this gathering, I knew, would be important. She is now one of the last elders on Kodiak who speak Alutiiq and carry with them knowledge of subsistence practices, healing and ethnobotany, basket making, and other arts. Betty Nelson from Port Lions and several other Kodiak elders contributed a great deal to the conference discussions. But it was Mary who took the microphone and responded when a young woman from Pilot Point stood, identified herself through her lineage, and sought permission to query the elders about their lives. The girl, initially nervous, summoned up her courage and asked what kind of foods had been fed to babies in earlier times.

Mary opened her response with "Cama'i," the Alutiiq greeting, and proceeded to talk about traditional pacifiers made from cheesecloth, describing how mothers would chew their food before giving it to infants. She told stories of her youth, of the migrations that had scattered Kodiak's people, and instructed the young people present to preserve the traditional ways of "being Aleut." The Monday following the conference, the *Kodiak Daily Mirror* pictured Mary on the front page with the caption "Elder shares her wit and wisdom." Truly, her confidence, eloquence, and humor marked her as an extraordinary public performer.[22]

Later, I talked with Mary about the changes in her life. During our final interviews, we discussed how she has experienced her later years, including menopause, and what it means to her to be an elder, especially with Larry Matfay and so many others gone.

*I still feel like the younger generations, until all of a sudden it hit me—seventy-one! Seventy-one! I had to say it several times. I can't believe it, you know. My cousins from Chignik said, "You're our only elder now." All of our elders are gone, and then Ignatius Kaspur just passed away not too long ago. He was my dad's relative, my great-auntie's brother.*

*I remember way back, we always respected our elders. To me, it seemed like when I was younger that they were like our children. We had to take care of them. They took care of us, so when they get older, it's our turn to take care of them. I used to clean their potties, or their spittoons; when they needed something washed, I'd go do that. It wasn't like today, having a washing machine. There's so much the old people want to do, and they can't. I just feel so sorry for them, you know. Their minds are working lots, but when they go to do some-thing, sometimes they can't. Like Anastasia Farsovitch—she was our elder in Akhiok—she wanted to do so much. She tried, but it's a good thing somebody was there. I used to go and see her all the time be-cause she liked somebody who spoke Aleut to visit. When I wasn't busy in the clinic, I'd go and see her, find out if she had dinner, and if she didn't, I'd make some Aleut food. I'd have a hard time leaving her, but finally I'd say I have to go home and cook now.*

*Nowadays, the kids all play Nintendo. I tell them to help them-selves, instead of getting someone else to do for them or somebody helping them. They waste their time with watching TV or playing those yucky Nintendo games. I hate those things! Even the moms get into them now, and they don't do their kitchen work and other things. They're too busy with Nintendo. They tried to teach me, and I said, "No way." I wouldn't get sewing or crocheting or baskets made.*

*Now, my kids are in the village—David, my son, and his wife, Luba, my son Mitchell and Judy and their kids, Albert and Diana and his kids, Walter Jr., my youngest boy, and my brother Lawrence. And the ones who never want me to go anywhere are Laurie Ann, my daughter, and Mary Lynn, my granddaughter. They always say, "Nanny, don't go no place" . . . and then the other ones, too, my oldest daughter's grandkids. I say, "I'll see you when I come to Kodiak." My daughter Judy is there, too.*

*And Mary Lynn, the last funeral we had in the village, it was Anastasia, it really hurt her. She asked her mom, "Are they gonna take grandma like that, too?" And Laurie Ann said, "Yeah, all of us. All of us will be laying like that when God is ready for us. When he's ready for us, he'll come and get us regardless of medicine and doctors. He's stronger than the doctors, and we can't help it. Grandma's getting old. She won't be with us all the time, you know." Mary Lynn was crying, "But not yet, Mom, not yet." Oh, gee, that just made me cry. I couldn't get good for a long time.*

*I don't know how many grandkids I have now. The last time we did count them down was in the '80s. My mom had sixty then, and I had forty something, and there are many more now. And I have one great-great—my daughter Vera, the oldest, her daughter, Jennie's daughter, Yolanda, had a baby, Devon—my great-great-grandson.*

*I miss having babies. When my younger ones were having babies, I just hurt in some way, someplace. I wished it was me. I never had problems delivering, and I never paid much attention to being pregnant. It never felt like it was in the way. My mom delivered eighteen kids, and I delivered eighteen kids, too. All of them didn't live. The older I was getting, my body was getting weaker.*

*I stopped having my period with a kidney problem [after a hysterectomy]. Otherwise, I would have had to have major surgery done on my kidneys, and they didn't know what complications would come up. I just told them I didn't want to. Then, two years ago, they tried to start me on estrogen. I wouldn't trust it. I just looked at it, then read the paper, and I said, "No, thank you. I'm doing just fine." I've been sweating now at night, and I'm used to it. All I have to do is drink lots of water, and that's what I do. I drink lots of juice, and I have a pitcher of Kool-Aid with the water and juices. If I sweat in the daytime, it's usually from working. Or sometimes, if I get nervous, I just break out sweating.*

*I take Tums because they have lots of calcium. Summertime, I quit taking my vitamins because we eats lots of fish, and that has iron. Only when I start to notice that we're not getting different foods, then I start taking my one-a-day vitamins without iron. If I start to feel low, I go and get them to check me for iron. If it's too low, even a bit, then I take the vitamins with iron. For some of us, iron is not good. Not one person is like another! Outside stuff—maybe you like the table to be like this, maybe I do, too—can be the same. Maybe two people might be in their looks but not in their actions and living ways. And not the human body. That's why some medicines that work for someone else don't work for me.*

I asked Mary what these elder/youth gatherings meant to her. Her responses referred back to the kinship workshop, when she'd discovered her Native last name as well as uncovered lost relatives. Her feeling that only Larry Matfay could truly confirm her name reveals the faith she places in oral tradition.

*Last year was the first time that other villagers were brought together. Before, in the old days, they did that by skiff. Last year, one old man, real tall man named John Pestrikoff, he met Nina Zeedar, and she told him that he was part of us from Kaguyak. Same way with someone from Karluk who moved to Kaguyak, and he became part of*

*Kaguyak, too. Things you find out! Maybe someone has more stories about Akhiok even than those of us who live there. That first day [of the conference], someone, I think it was Roy Madsen, who said, "Tomorrow's going to be the day that we find out who's who and where they're from." You might be sitting at the same table with someone and not even know you're cousins.*

*One woman who had that computer, she looked up "Teacon Peterson" and found the name "Chumlumloo" at the end. Frank Peterson's wife, Joyce, she said, "Yeah, that was your dad's real last name—'Chumlumloo.'" I don't know because now Larry Matfay is gone. He was the one who really knew who I was, where I was born, and what year I was born. He said that I'm just a few years younger than the church in Akhiok. It was built almost the same year that I was born. Now Larry's gone, and the only way to find out is through the computer.*

Mary also repeated two stories I'd heard before, establishing her connection to Akhiok as the place where she "belongs" and reiterating how much better her birthing experiences had been with midwives. In this context, she linked "belonging" with the work of the midwife, affirming the place of this pivotal figure in Kodiak's history and in the reproduction of cultural as well as biological life.

*I'm used to Peterson now. I don't know how I would feel about it [the new name]. Simeonoff [her second husband's name] wasn't our real last name, either. Walter's real name was "Kagik." The kids said, "I wish our name was 'Kagik,' because it's easier to write and shorter . . . We could feel like we belong." I don't know how they could get that feeling that they don't belong. I said, "I'm not understanding this now. You still belong to Akhiok because you were born here. Most of my kids were born here, except for the ones that died in the hospital. I told the nurses, "You know what? All my children that lived were delivered by midwives in the village, even down to a two-pound, thirteen ounce baby . . . And those two, Sophia and Nick, they were born in the hospital and you didn't make them live." And I said, "You know why? Because you didn't stay with the baby all night like our midwives in the village did."*

Mary's final words at the elders/youth conference reaffirmed a theme she badly wanted to communicate to young people that day—the "believing" central to her life story. After she'd spoken to the group for more than forty minutes about traditional child rearing, transformations in village life, and the importance of community, she stopped all at once, with a look of panic.

*I think I'm taking too much time. Just like Larry Matfay, once I get started, I don't know when to quit. Larry used to tell me, "No matter what, there's only one person who belongs in your heart besides your loved ones—our Lord in Heaven." You know by the cross [holding up a gold double-barred Russian Orthodox cross around her neck] that you're one of his children. He's the only thing that shines in us, like the stars shine, like your rings shine. Just like you put a stamp on a letter or you mark anything you own and say, "That belongs to me," that's how we are to our Lord in Heaven. No matter where you go or what you do, don't forget to wear your cross. Wear it in your heart.*

When Mary held up her cross, I remembered the ways that "healing" and "belief" had crossed over in her words again and again and how integral Russian Orthodoxy was to their juncture. When

I consider what Mary has endured in her life—violence, multiple losses, the battle to sustain Alutiiq culture—I wonder at the strength of her belief and the absence of rancor in her words. I remember a letter in which she wrote, "When I talk to my grown-up kids now, I try to talk about the happy times I had during my growing up and adult life. And I say I wish I was back in those days now. And my kids say, 'Why Mom? It sounds like it was hard.' I say, 'Hard? No, now it's hard . . . Before, it was like one big family and everyone helped each other.'" The narrative of community life, the attendant values of sharing and reciprocity, the very definition of "being Aleut" override whatever Mary has suffered because that is the story she chooses to tell and, in that telling, to contribute to the re-creation of Alutiiq culture today.

When Mary finished speaking that bright September day, everyone in the room rose for an extended standing ovation. The crowd nearly eclipsed Mary's tiny frame, but through the cracks in the wall of people I could see that she was smiling. Her niece Irene Coyle broke the applause by taking the microphone to call attention once again to Mary's life as exemplary. I expected a reference to her spiritual strength, her knowledge of tradition, her service to the community, but, as a final tribute, Irene exclaimed joyfully, "She's seventy-one years old, and last night she outdanced me!"

# Epilogue

By the end of the twentieth century a majority of children born to Kodiak Natives were delivered by Western doctors at the Kodiak Island Hospital or in Anchorage. As Mary states, "Nowadays, the new generation, they'd rather go to the hospital. When I was the midwife, I started thinking, 'If anything went wrong, I'd be to blame for not sending her to the hospital in Kodiak, instead of trying to risk helping her to give birth.'" Midwifery among Kodiak Natives is a historical phenomenon, replaced by Western medical practices. Yet stories of healing and midwifery continue to be told—in the villages, in *banyas* and homes, and at the increasing number of elders' conferences held among Alutiiq and other Native peoples.

Why do they matter? The stories Mary Peterson tells offer a unique perspective on both historical and contemporary issues, including the evolution of women's healing roles. Despite some excellent anthropological studies, there remains a dearth of information about women and health care.[1] Further, some of the contemporary popular books about Native healers romanticize and simplify their lives. Real lives brim with pain and trauma as well as wisdom and insight. We need their full unfolding for an understanding of history.

Also central to Mary's story is the meaning of "being Aleut," opening new windows onto ethnic identity, in this case, of a people long neglected in anthropological and popular literature. The anthropologist Hugh Brody has noted a similar neglect of the people in northeast British Columbia, an area overlooked by scholars in their haste to find a vision of the "Arctic splendor and space . . . the region of the real, supposedly untouched hunters of the Far North."[2] Alutiiq people, long in contact with non-Natives, have had to rethink and reinterpret their culture again and again. The patterns they've achieved tell us much about the process of interpreting ethnicity, re-creating culture, and "healing."

For Kodiak Natives, "healing" has meant to rebuild community, to banish violence and alcohol abuse, to reclaim and reinvent a culture. Alutiiq identity was not excavated intact from burial but rather negotiated in ongoing interaction with local, national, and global political movements. Events of the past two decades have tightened the bonds between Kodiak's people and other Alutiiqs; the 1991 repatriation of burial remains to Larsen Bay from the Smithsonian Institution focused national attention on Kodiak, and international researchers from Scandinavia and Russia have visited the island to explore ethnic identity.

The term *Alutiiq* now rolls with ease off people's tongues in long overdue recognition of a culture decreed "dead" twenty years ago. The Alutiiq Museum and Archaeological Repository stands at the center of Kodiak, and Alutiiq culture figures prominently in school curricula. One Alutiiq Museum bulletin, which arrived in my mailbox in 1999, advertises two "traveling educational boxes"—"Who are the Alutiiq?" and "An Alutiiq Education: Toys, Games, and Stories." These explore Native heritage with hands-on activities, taped vocabulary lessons, and an interactive time line.

Elsewhere, the bulletin calls for participants at the Kodiak Area Native Association's Youth "Spirit Camp" on nearby Sitkalidik Island, featuring practical skills such as wilderness survival as well as "talking circles"—a "safe environment to talk about sensitive issues." Once a week, a lesson in Alutiiq language "Alutiiq Word of the Week" appears on my e-mail screen; the same lesson is broadcast on Kodiak Public Radio KMXT and published in the *Kodiak Daily Mirror*.

In Akhiok, Alutiiq cultural transformation is evident in daily life. The village is a far safer and more inviting place than it was in the 1980s, when I first traveled there. Community celebrations, "starring," and religious practices are again integrated into the yearly cycle. The current population has grown to 108 people. Even during lean fishing years, residents strive to find work and stay in the village. Mary's son Mitchell and his wife, Judy, started an adventure-tour business to draw visitors to the south end of the island. The oft-invoked "healing" does indeed seem to be underway.

Yet when I called Mary just before Mothers' Day 1999, I realized how incomplete and ongoing the healing process is. I'd been trying to reach her for months as she traveled back and forth between Kodiak and Anchorage. Two deaths had added to the succession of losses in her life. En route to Disneyland with her grandchildren in March, she stopped in Anchorage to discover that her eldest daughter, Vera, had died. Later, when she told me about the death, she said, "We didn't even know she was sick. She didn't want to worry anyone. I just hurt for those kids, my grandkids and great-grandkids. I just hurt for them." Mary had barely recovered from one funeral when her ex-husband, Walter, died in the village. Her youngest daughter, Laurie Ann, found him. "She went to pick up his garbage, and she thought he was just sleeping. She tried to wake him, but he was already stiff. They had to take her to the clinic. She was in shock." A silence filled the telephone line. "I just got home, and now it's just grieving."

When I spoke to Mary two months later, she was stronger, despite the additional loss of her sister's husband and a scare when her brother Lawrence had to be flown out of the village with pneumonia. Mary described her fears of another death. "At first I said, 'Oh, no, not again,' but then I just prayed hard. I said, 'Just hold on. I can't break down now or I'll make myself sick.'" Facing crisis, Mary turned, as she has throughout her life, to her sources of sustenance—church, family, tradition. Though the village reader, Ephraim Agnot, is dead, Luba, Mary's daughter-in-law, has carried on in his place, chanting the liturgy under brilliant icons. When we spoke, Mary was preparing for a summer of salmon fishing at her fish camp, picking grasses for basket making, planning to crochet blankets for one of her many grandchildren. She looked again to the "medicine from the land," saying, "I take it every summer, even if I'm not sick. If I wait, I might get sick. But I know it works, because I believe." During our telephone conversation, Mary told a story I'd heard several times before about how her kidney infection had healed from "land medicine" and treatment by Oleanna Ashouwak, repeated in a new context to recall the strength of tradition.

But the traditions Mary describes as central to her life are not static. The anthropologist Dell Hymes suggests we think of tradition as a process rather than simply naming objects and practices, as a verb rather than a noun.[3] We "traditionalize" our experience to make meaning of our everyday lives, to ritualize and mark what we hold sacred, to help us survive loss and suffering. In this sense, tradition is constantly selected and created as a "conscious model of past lifeways that people use in the construction of their identity."[4] For Akhiok villagers, culture must serve contemporary interests. Today, village children carve a kayak, not for fishing, as their ancestors did, but to remind them of who they are, ritually re-creating ancestral spirit. One of the strongest tools in this process is the storytelling that sustains the Alutiiq people. In Western culture, we often denigrate "mere" stories, elevating a more public, abstract discourse that the writer Ursula LeGuin calls the "father tongue." But for Native people, stories have long offered central truths. Leslie Marmon Silko, a Laguna Pueblo novelist and storyteller, reminds us in her novel *Ceremony* that stories are "not just entertainment. Don't be fooled. They are all we have, you see. You don't have anything if you don't have the stories." Among contemporary writers, N. Scott Momaday, Leslie Marmon Silko, Paula Gunn Allen, Rayna Green, and Peter Kalifornsky all point to stories as a distinct way of knowing.

Narratives about Native midwives matter for what they teach about history, ethnicity, healing, and women's lives. But they also matter as *stories*, illuminating much about the meaning and changing context of both traditional and personal narrative. Stories flow through the embankment of history, but its boundaries are not as rigid as they appear. Stories push against the walls that seem to contain them, remaking the very landscape in their wake. As the anthropologist Julie Cruikshank describes it, "narrative and history reciprocally shape one another."[5] Stories shift with each subsequent telling and for each audience, a reminder of Walter Benjamin's notion that whereas information "exhausts itself," stories are endlessly generative.[6] Mary's storytelling at the 1993 gathering of the Alaska Maternal Child Health Coalition had different contours than that of the interviews I'd conducted in private. At the conference, she shaped her stories in connection to and collaboration with other midwives and adapted them to the contemporary needs of the women in attendance.

Succeeding generations of women also alter the form and content of received stories. At a 1988 women's conference in Kodiak, one session focused on women healers and midwives. There, several younger women told the same narratives I'd heard from Mary—tales of Oleanna Ashouwak, stories that stressed the importance of the midwives and the Community Health Aides. But they spoke without the religious overtones that colored Mary's and other older women's stories, which often attributed healing power to spiritual "knowing" received from God. Rather, a new generation openly expressed a preference for treatment by a Native healer for medical reasons quite apart from religious inspiration, a shift influenced by the growing Native revitalization movement. Some of the younger women told humorous stories as well. One described a dentist who, while living in one of the villages, had tried to deliver a baby, finally calling the Native midwife in desperation. Despite differences in content and tone, stories of both generations emphasize the centrality of women's healing roles, practically and symbolically. Both sets of narratives point to the need to see stories as socially shaped and, in turn, as shapers of society.

These stories, as well as the material culture and artifacts of Alutiiq culture, will garner statewide attention in 2000. The museum staff is working with the Arctic Studies Center (Smithsonian Institution) in Anchorage on the project "Looking Both Ways: Heritage and Identity of the Alutiiq People." This community-based project involves educational programs and a two-year traveling exhibit. The project directors sought input from elders at the 1997 and 1998 Alutiiq elders/youth gatherings, highlighting the importance of having local people control cultural representation. The exhibit combines oral histories, ethnographic items, photos, and artifacts from the Alutiiq Museum and from the National Museum of Natural History in Washington, DC. "Looking Both Ways" chronicles the Alutiiq past as well as the bright future promised by the good health of village communities, by increased awareness of ethnic identity, and by the continued rebirth of the culture. The stories about how and what Native women "knew" remain essential, a cornerstone in rebuilding the cultural heritage of Kodiak's Native people.

Stories, writes N. Scott Momaday, "are predicated upon belief. Belief is more essential to the story than is understanding . . . In my story, I create a state of being in which you are immediately involved." Belief, the core of Mary's worldview, draws in whoever listens to her stories, making us all "immediately involved." There are multiple audiences for Mary's words: local and national, Native and non-Native, healers and patients, and the extended kinship network so central to her life. Above all, it's for her grandchildren and great-grandchildren, Mary says, that she wants her story told and traditional knowledge carried on, "so that they can have really good lives. For them, I want the best."

# Notes

## Introduction

1. Archaeologists have divided Kodiak's cultural traditions into five periods. Flaked stone tools and barbed harpoon heads marked the Ocean Bay period (c. 5500 to 2500 B.C.); slate implements, new fish harvesting techniques, and carved stone lamps developed during the Kachemak phase (c. 2500 B.C. to A.D. 1200); the Koniag period followed from A.D. 1200 to 1784; the final two periods are the Russian era (1784–1867) and the American period (1867 to the present). There is debate among archaeologists as to how firm the division really is between the Kachemak and the Koniag phase. See Jordan and Knecht, "Archaeological Research," 356–453.

2. For histories and documentation of Russian America see Black, "Russian Conquest"; Davydov, *Voyages*; and Tikhmenev, *History*.

3. The "Creole" population that emerged from the intermarriage of Native women and Russian men grew to include all Native Alaskans who pledged allegiance to the tsar after 1821. Many were educated by the Orthodox monks who followed the fur traders to "Russian America" and established schools. Creoles were groomed for church, trade, or educational service, sometimes in Russia. They continued the development of literacy and founded schools. See Barbara Sweetland Smith, "Russia's Cultural Legacy in America: The Orthodox Mission," in *Russian America: The Forgotten Frontier*, ed. Barbara Sweetland Smith and Red-

mond J. Barnett, 245–53 (Tacoma: Washington State Historical Society, 1990); and Oleksa, "Creoles," 185–95.

4. The work of feminist scholars is too voluminous to review here, but to briefly note a few important works: For historical re-visioning of women's lives, see Nancy F. Cott and Elizabeth H. Peck, *A Heritage of Her Own: Toward a New Social History of American Women* (New York: Simon and Schuster, 1979); Armitage and Jameson, *Women's West*; and Gerda Lerner, *The Majority Finds Its Past: Placing Women in History* (New York: Oxford University Press, 1979). In anthropology, two seminal texts are Rayna Reiter, ed., *Toward an Anthropology of Women* (New York: Monthly Review Press, 1975); and Michelle Simbalist Rosaldo and Louise Lamphere, eds., *Women, Culture, and Society* (Stanford, Calif.: Stanford University Press, 1974). For analyses of women's stories, see Jordan and Kalčik, *Women's Folklore*; Radner, *Feminist Messages*; Personal Narratives Group, *Women's Lives*; and Gluck and Patai, *Women's Words*.

5. Although a number of archaeologists have worked on Kodiak throughout this century, there is a dearth of cultural ethnographies. Some noteworthy exceptions are the work of Nancy Yaw Davis, Rachel Mason, Craig Mishler, and the Native scholar Gordon Pullar.

6. See Sidney Mintz, foreword to *African-American Anthropology: Contemporary Perspectives*, ed. Norman E. Whitten Jr. and John F. Szwed, 1–16 (New York: Free Press, 1970). In *Eskimo Essays*, Ann Fienup-Riordan similarly explores how the contemporary Yup'ik create and reinterpret tradition. Both draw on current theoretical shifts away from essentialist notions of culture to dynamic models of innovation and invention. See also James Clifford, *The Predicament of Culture: Twentieth-Century Ethnography, Literature, and Art* (Cambridge: Harvard University Press, 1988); and Eric Hobswam and Terence Ranger, eds., *The Invention of Tradition* (Cambridge: Cambridge University Press, 1983).

7. Life histories form a long tradition in anthropology and folklore research. For an overview, see Langness and Frank, *Lives*. In particular,

this tradition has focused on Native American life histories. See Bataille and Sands, *American Indian Women*; Blackman, *During My Time*; Bodfish, *Kusig*; Moses Cruikshank, *The Life I've Been Living*; and Julie Cruikshank, *Life Lived Like a Story*. For other cultural comparisons, see Behar, *Translated Woman*; Vincent Crapanzano, *Tuhami*; Gmelch, *Nan*; and Shostak, *Nisa*.

8. In many life histories, personal narratives, that is stories told as accounts the individual experienced, often overlap with oral tradition, stories that are handed down, shaped in social interaction, and retold. See Stahl, "Personal Narrative"; Schrager, "Oral History"; and Titon, "Life Story." For specific considerations of oral tradition in the north, see Morrow and Schneider, *When Our Words Return*.

9. For the classic literature on revitalization movements, see Wallace, "Revitalization Movements"; Wallace, "Revitalization Processes"; and Linton, "Nativistic Movements." Following Linton, Gordon Pullar characterizes the movement on Kodiak as "revivalistic" and "magical" in that the "focus of today's movement is on strengthening the spiritual connection with one's heritage and sense of identity rather than on reclaiming certain rights." See Pullar, "Ethnic Identity," 182–91.

10. Katz and Craig, "Community Healing."

11. Turner, "Traditional Healing." See also Turner, *The Hands Feel It*.

12. Napoleon, *Yuuyaraq*.

13. See Chamberlain, "Telling Tales."

14. Dwyer argues for a presentation of ethnographic interviews in dialogue form, but I found this too disruptive to Mary's narrative. I have inserted questions only when it seemed necessary for clarification. See Dwyer, "Dialogue." Hymes, Tedlock, and others argue for the use of visual formats and poetic form to recreate features of speech and patterns of language, particularly with traditional texts. See Hymes, "*In Vain*"; and Tedlock, *Spoken Word*.

15. For discussions of oral and literate cultures, see Ong, *Orality*; and Goody, *Domestication*.

16. De Laurentis, "Essence." For anthropological views, see Behar,

*Vulnerable Observer*; and see Behar's introduction to *Translated Woman* for a discussion of the social boundaries she had to "translate" in her fashioning of a Mexican woman's life history. See also Lila Abu-Lughod, *Writing Women's Worlds* (Berkeley: University of California Press, 1993), 5. Abu-Lughod documents two sources of tension and inequality between "self" and "other" in conducting and writing feminist anthropology: that of the feminist studying women and that of the usually Western anthropologist analyzing non-Western lives.

17. In 1989, Kodiak's first cultural heritage conference focused the attention of scholars and museum specialists from Europe, Russia, and the Smithsonian Institution on Kodiak's culture and the removal of art and artifacts over the course of over two centuries. In 1991, human remains and grave goods taken from the village of Larsen Bay by the Czech anthropologist Aleš Hrdlička were repatriated from the Smithsonian, one of the largest such cases in American history. Thus, a history of "plundering" has particular significance and sensitivity for Kodiak Natives. See Bray and Killian, *Reckoning*.

## The Early Seasons

### Family

1. Naming practices, linguist Jeff Leer suggested at the Alutiiq conference, revealed the multiple layerings so evident in Alutiiq culture: American practices blended with Russian traditions, both overlaid onto ancient Alutiiq names. The family names Mary refers to here, especially "Signuk" and "Kagik," had appeared in print earlier, in kinship data and in census reports, with alternate spellings. "Kagik" also appears as "Kegik"; Mary's mother's name, "Ephrezenea," is also spelled "Ephrazinnia." Other variations frequently occur.

2. After the U.S. purchase of Alaska in 1867, a number of industries were developed on Kodiak, including cattle ranching, trapping, fox farm-

ing, and gold mining. Some fox farms were owned by trading companies that hired Native men to hunt and fish to provide food for the foxes; other Natives worked independently, selling the fox skins to the traders. See Mason, "Alutiiq Ethnographic Bibliography," 17.

3. *Barabaras* (*ciqlluaqs* in Alutiiq) were used until the mid-twentieth century in the villages; photographs from the 1960s show the last *barabara* used in the village of Old Harbor. In the 1980s, several were built in Akhiok and other villages as part of traditional arts programs set up to ensure that young villagers have a sense of their own history and culture, and as part of programs to counter alcoholism and social problems in the villages.

Being Aleut

4. Linguists refer to Kodiak's native language as "Suk," "Sugpiaq," "Sugcestun," or "Pacific Yupik." "Alutiiq" is now also used for the language as well as the culture. See Michael Krauss, "Many Tongues—Ancient Tales," in *Crossroads of Continents*, ed. William Fitzhugh and Aaron Crowell, 145–50 (Washington, D.C.: Smithsonian Institution Press, 1988).

5. See Jordan and Knecht, "Archaeological Research"; and Townsend, "Ranked Societies." For a discussion of Alutiiq ceremonial life, see Donta, "Continuity and Function."

6. "Aleut," writes the Native scholar Gordon Pullar, "originated in Siberia as 'Aliutor,' a name applied to a coastal indigenous group on the Kamchatka Peninsula. Russian explorers thought the people they encountered in Alaska were the same." Though "Aleut" was adopted as the vernacular self-reference, scholars continued to classify Kodiak's people as Pacific Eskimo divided into three subgroups: The Chugachmiut (Prince William Sound), the Unegkurmiut (lower Kenai Peninsula), and the Koniagmiut (Kodiak Island area and the Alaska Peninsula). For an overview of the Pacific Eskimo, see Davis, "Contemporary Pacific Eskimo," 198–204. For an analysis of how the term "Aleut" evolved, see

Oleksa, "Kodiak Island Natives," and *Alaska Missionary Spirituality* (Mahwah, N.J.: Paulist Press, 1987).

7. Although culturally Kodiak Natives share more with the Yup'ik Eskimo than with the Aleutian Islanders, many of the Kodiak elders I met adamantly insisted they were "not Eskimo." The anthropologist Ann Fienup-Riordan points to the long-standing "etymological confusion" about the term "Eskimo." The name originated in Montagnais form meaning "snowshoe netter"; however, for nearly a century, dictionaries as well as the general public have traced the word to an Algonquian root meaning "eaters of raw flesh." Fienup-Riordan argues that the pervasive view of Eskimos as the "ultimate natural men" has helped perpetuate the error. Perhaps the pejorative term "flesh eaters" contributed to Kodiak Natives' feeling about the term "Eskimo." See Fienup-Riordan, *Eskimo Essays*.

8. Annual Medical Report from Dr. Orr to the Bureau of Education, 12 June 1913, National Archives, Washington, D.C.

9. See Robert Alberts, "A Village Re-Awakening," *Alaska Native News*, May–June 1984.

10. See Fischer, "Ethnicity"; Fishman, *Rise and Fall*; and Sollors, *Beyond Ethnicity*.

11. I am grateful to the anthropologist Patricia Partnow for her discussions of Alutiiq identity on the Alaska Peninsula; several distinct characteristics of those communities relate as well to Kodiak. See Patricia Partnow, "Ethnicity in the Twentieth Century: The Alutiiq Case" (paper presented at the Alaska Anthropological Meeting, Juneau, Alaska, March 1994).

12. Mary sometimes calls crowberries (*Empetrum nigrum*) "blackberries."

13. Material objects and figurines found by archaeologists suggest that shamans utilized spirit figures for good and ill purposes. Spirits were believed to be ancestors who had either become evil or had achieved greater status in the supernatural world. See Donta, "Continuity," 125.

14. I have merged two stories about shamans here, one Mary told me in an interview, and one she told at the 1998 elders/youth gathering in Kodiak. Other elders told similar stories about shamans. Lucille Davis described the shamans' use of dolls for ritual purposes, how the children had to wash their hands if they touched them, and how people feared their powers. Other elders spoke about the replacement of the shaman by the priest and traditional Russian Orthodox beliefs.

Faith

15. See Oleksa, "Kodiak Island Natives"; and Oleksa, "Three Saints Bay."

16. "Selaviq" originated in the sixteenth century in the Carpathian Mountains of the Ukraine. It began as a way to maintain local religious practice in the face of the forced Latinization of the Russian Orthodox Church and is now practiced in varied ways by different Native communities. "Starring" still involves feasting at each house that the carolers visit, and often the giving of gifts. This has led the anthropologist Ann Fienup-Riordan to describe the event in the Yukon-Kuskokwim Delta area as a "ritual distribution, community celebration, and religious holiday all rolled into one." See Fienup-Riordan, "Following the Star."

17. See Mishler, "The Nuta'aq."

18. Mishler argues in "The Nuta'aq" that in English Bay a similar drama symbolically plays out tensions between whites and Natives. Different communities adapt the tradition to cultural needs and change.

19. See Mishler, "Aurcaq." Mishler's recent documentation of this game in the village of Old Harbor suggests these interpretations, although many of the elders describe the game as a means of recreation.

20. Since the 1960s, lay readers, now most often women, have become more involved in general community life. Rachel Mason has traced the evolution of the role during the two hundred years since Russian clergy arrived on Kodiak in 1794. See Mason, "Russian Orthodox Church Readers."

School

21. For overviews of Russian Orthodox education on Kodiak, see Oleksa, " Creoles," and Smith, "Russia's Cultural Legacy."

22. See Adams, *Education*, 14.

23. Cited in Adams, *Education*, 19. He notes that not all philanthropists of the era concurred that Indians were educable; dissenters adhered to the philosophy of the "inherent inferiority" of Indians to whites.

24. See Robinson, *Education*. Many Kodiak elders I interviewed had fond memories of attending the Russian mission school in Kodiak.

25. For educational reports, see the Bureau of Indian Affairs records, National Archives and Records Service, Washington, D.C., record group 75, box 61: *1916 Annual Report Akhiok School*, record group drawer 143, file 357, folder 1915–1917, Akhiok school; and folder 1934–1950, "Village school descriptions, health records, food survey, and census data."

26. For additional memories of the Akhiok school, see Michael Rostad's biography of the elder Larry Matfay, *Time to Dance*, 25–29. Rostad uses the spelling "Sellars," but I am following references in the National Archives to a Kathryn D. Seller writing from the village in 1920, and in 1939 census data.

Work

27. For a discussion of the mother's brother's role in contemporary society that supports the argument for matrilineality, see Davis, "Sociocultural Description."

28. For an overview of salmon fishing in Alaska, see Roppel, *Salmon Hatcheries*.

Coming of Age

29. Holmberg, *Ethnographic Sketches*, cited in Fortuine's *Chills and Fever*, 11.

30. See the introduction to Gottlieb and Buckley, *Blood Magic*, for an excellent overview of cross-cultural studies of menstruation.

31. Mary Douglas provides an analysis of women outside the social order who are both dangerous and powerful that is particularly related to menstrual blood and miscarriage; see Douglas, *Purity and Danger*. Also see Emily Martin's analysis of the metaphors of reproduction in Martin, *The Woman in the Body: A Cultural Analysis of Reproduction* (Boston: Beacon Press, 1987).

32. Julie Cruikshank offers an analysis of Native women's experiences that compares with that of women on Kodiak. Cruikshank notes that, for the three Yukon elders with whom she worked, puberty seclusion was a time for acquiring ritual and practical knowledge unavailable to men. She contrasts this view with conventional assertions that women were perceived as "polluted" during these periods. See Julie Cruikshank, *Life Lived Like a Story*, 11.

33. Interview by author with Clyda Christensen, 7 November 1985.

Marriage

34. Robert Fortuine describes a 1934 study that found that 35.5 percent of Native deaths in a five-year period were due to tuberculosis. Although awareness of how critical the situation was continued to grow, World War II disrupted and delayed the building of hospitals closer to home for many Natives. See Fortuine, "Health Care," 13.

## Women and Healing

Midwifery and Traditional Health Care

1. *Berdache* is the more general term for a "third gender" role referred to in ethnographic accounts as "transvestite," "shopan" or "achnucek." See Williams, *Spirit*.

2. For Russian accounts of traditional healing, see Lisiansky, *Voyage*, 185; and Davydov, *Two Voyages*, 178.

3. See Fortuine, *Chills and Fever*, 194.

4. Interview by author with Dr. Bob Johnson in Kodiak, 7 August 1985.

5. Fortuine, "Health Care," 8.

6. Bureau of Education Reports, 8 August 1913; and 1917, National Archives, Washington, D.C., record group 75, box 61.

7. "Taaritet," the plural of "taarin," is often used for a single scrubber, since it refers to a bunch of grass roots. The linguist Jeff Leer pointed out to me that in other dialects "taaritet" refers to the *banya* switches, not the scrubbers.

8. For cross-cultural comparisons of birthing systems, see Kay, *Anthropology*; and Brigitte Jordan, *Birth*.

9. The notion of blindness as sacred figured prominently in mythology and literature previous to the rise of a scientific worldview. The Enlightenment association of ideas and knowledge as based on perceptions and sensations "desacrilized" this symbol. See Paulson, *Enlightenment*.

10. Interviews by author with Nida Chya on 5 August 1985 and with Clyda Christensen on 7 November 1985.

11. Bureau of Education Report, 1917.

The Community Health Aide System

12. See Parran et al., *Alaska's Health*.

13. See *Alaska CHA Program Description*, 1980, 1991. For a history of the CHA Program, see Nice with Johnson, *Alaska Health Aide Program*.

14. The Alaska Native Claims Settlement Act (ANCSA) created thirteen Native corporations (twelve in Alaska and one for Alaska Natives living outside the state). These regional corporations, with additional funding from the Indian Health Service (IHS) and the state of Alaska, hire and pay CHAs; since the 1975 Indian Self-Determination and Education Assistance Act, some villages now contract their health care out to private providers. See *Alaska CHA Program Description*, 1991.

15. I refer to CHAs throughout because it is the term Mary uses. However, many CHAs now become certified CHPs (Community Health Practitioners). This requires successful completion of a basic training of

four sessions (three of four weeks' duration, one of three weeks'), a clinical skills preceptorship, and a qualifying exam.

16. Telephone interview by author, 12 September 1999.

17. "Risk" must be considered within a cultural context. Older women's stories of the midwives' "knowing" were told as part of a worldview that saw birth as a community process sometimes accompanied by loss. With increasing westernization has come the dominant model of childbirth as a "high risk" process best aided by technology. For a general treatment of technology and birth in America, see Davis-Floyd, *Birth*.

18. Amy Steffian pointed out to me that this story echoes the Alutiiq creation myth recorded by Lisiansky in which wood chips thrown into the water turn to fish, an example of the synthesis of Alutiiq and Russian Orthodox culture. See Lisiansky, *Voyage*.

Memories of Oleanna Ashouwak

19. Interview by author with Rena Cohen, Akhiok, Alaska, 21 October 1985.

20. Interview by author with Stella Stanley, Old Harbor, Alaska, 15 October 1986.

21. Several people compared the work of Oleanna Ashouwak to the better-known Della Keats. Keats, an Inupiat healer celebrated throughout Alaska before her death in 1986, successfully integrated traditional and modern medicine. Her use of massage, "poking" to let blood, steambaths, hot springs, and spirituality is remarkably like Oleanna's. See Juul, "Portrait."

22. Aleš Hrdlička cites the Russian priest Father Veniaminov's observation of something akin to Oleanna Ashouwak's practice of "holding": "If the patient feels gnawing or anguish in the abdomen, or something similar, they lay him on his back, and a woman with both hands holds his abdomen, gently manipulating with her fingers his internal parts, for the purpose they say, to bring them into order, laying everything where it belongs" (Hrdlička, *Anthropology*, 177).

23. Sasha is the pseudonym of a woman I interviewed in 1985.

24. Myths allow for such complex contradiction. The anthropologist Susan Harding writes that the myths women tell tend "not to resolve their complication, just to raise it," suggesting that "the contradictions which they treat, like the contradictions embedded in the lives of women, are not solved." See Harding, "Women and Words," 297.

25. See Lisiansky, *Voyage*; Davydov, *Two Voyages*; and Fortune, *Chills and Fever*.

26. For women's position in healing and ritual roles, see McClain, *Women as Healers*, 6–7; and Brettell and Sargent, "Gender, Ritual, and Religion," in Brettell and Sargent, *Gender*, 351–55.

27. Samuel and Thompson, *Myths*, 19.

## Exile and Renewal

### Change in Akhiok

1. Bill Schneider pointed out to me that many of the social problems villagers face spring from "conflicting images of the good life," from the difficulties of pursuing traditional ways in a modern context, and from living in two or more worlds. Schneider, personal communication, 1999.

2. For the history of alcohol in Alaska, see Fortune, *Chills and Fever*, 279–99.

3. In 1976, a group of volunteers founded the Kodiak Women's Resource Center (KWRC). When I joined the staff in 1979, we ran a crisis line from a church basement. The next decade saw increased funding and inclusion in a statewide network of women's organizations. New educational and violence prevention programs and extended outreach to the villages followed. Initially, villagers were reluctant to accept outsiders' services. Gradually, in cooperation with the Kodiak Area Native Association, village women began to use the KWRC. The center, now called the Kodiak Women's Resource and Crisis Center, has grown,

has built a shelter, and continues to provide important services on Kodiak.

A People in Peril

4. Howard Weaver, "A Deep Wound, Slow to Heal," *Anchorage Daily News*, 11 January 1988, A1.

5. See Pullar, "Ethnic Identity."

6. Cited by Weaver, "People in Peril."

The *Exxon Valdez* Oil Spill

7. Pullar, "Ethnic Identity."

8. For connections between the effects of the earthquake and the oil spill, see Davis, "Oil Spill." Also see Mason, *Final Report*.

9. Davis, "Oil Spill," 244.

10. Davis, "Oil Spill," 255.

Return to Akhiok

11. Dauenhauer and Dauenhauer, *Haa Shuka'*.

12. For a description of Aleut basketry and its influence on Kodiak basket makers, see Shapsnikoff and Hudson, "Aleut Basketry"; and Hudson, "Attu Weavers."

13. Eunice Neseth of Kodiak was widely acknowledged for her Attu basketry.

A Gathering of Midwives

14. The anthropologist Julie Cruikshank discusses the need for re-thinking contemporary contexts for storytelling, examining how First Nations people in Canada negotiate identities in new ways at storytelling festivals. See Julie Cruikshank, *Social Life*, 138–59.

15. Ong writes of how secondary orality is like primary orality in "its participatory mystique, its fostering of a communal sense, its concentration on the present moment, and even its use of formulas . . . But it is es-

sentially a more deliberate and self-conscious orality, based permanently on the use of writing and print, which are essential for the manufacture and operation of the equipment and for its use as well" (see Ong, *Orality*, 136–37).

16. Ong, *Orality*, 81.

Letters: 1993–1995

17. See Mulcahy with Peterson, "Mary Peterson"; and Mulcahy, "Dreams and Shadows."

Ways of Knowing

18. Kawagley, *Yupiaq World View*.

We Are One

19. The Alaska Native Claims Settlement Act (ANCSA) traded Native rights to the land for a settlement of nearly a billion dollars and forty-four million acres of land. This historic legislation ended decades of struggle by Native people for a clear definition of land use and policy; however, it also raised a score of troubling issues. Today, Native people are questioning the applicability of a corporate structure to Native life and reassessing the future of their land.

20. With ANCSA, Alutiiq villages were divided into three different regions. "In the short twenty years since the passage of ANCSA," writes Gordon Pullar, "the Alutiiq villages have come to identify more with their ANCSA region than with their culture area." See Pullar, "Proposal"; also see Arnold, *Land Claims*.

21. For a detailed description, see Fitzhugh and Crowell, *Crossroads*, 209.

22. Mary's self-assurance and stature mirrors that of older women in different cultures who gain such power as they age and move beyond child-rearing years. See Amoss and Harrell, *Other Ways*.

*Epilogue*

1. For a view of healing roles that combines them with a theoretical focus on gender, see McClain, *Women as Healers*.

2. Brody, *Maps and Dreams*.

3. See Dell Hymes, "Folklore's Nature and the Sun's Myth," *Journal of American Folklore* 88 (1975): 345–69.

4. Linnekin, "Defining Tradition," 241.

5. Julie Cruikshank, *Social Life*, 164.

6. Benjamin, "Storyteller."

# Bibliography

Adams, David Wallace. *Education for Extinction.* Lawrence: University Press of Kansas, 1995.

Afonsky, Bishop Gregory. *A History of the Orthodox Church in Alaska, (1794–1917).* Kodiak, Alaska: St. Herman's Theological Seminary, 1977.

*Alaska CHA Program Description.*: Alaska Area Native Health Service. Anchorage, 1980, 1991.

Amoss, Pamela T., and Stevan Harrell, eds. *Other Ways of Growing Old: Anthropological Perspectives.* Stanford, Calif.: Stanford University Press, 1981.

Armitage, Susan, and Elizabeth Jameson, eds. *The Women's West.* Norman: University of Oklahoma, 1987.

Arnold, Robert A. *Alaska Native Land Claims.* Anchorage: Alaska Native Foundation, 1976.

Bataille, Gretchen M., and Kathleen M. Sands. *American Indian Women: Telling Their Lives.* Lincoln: University of Nebraska Press, 1984.

Behar, Ruth. *Translated Woman.* Boston: Beacon Press, 1993.

———. *The Vulnerable Observer: Anthropology That Breaks Your Heart.* Boston: Beacon Press, 1996.

Ben-Amos, Dan. "The Seven Strands of Tradition: Varieties in Its Meaning in American Folklore Studies." *Journal of Folklore Research* 21, 2–3 (1984): 97–131.

151

Benjamin, Walter. "The Storyteller." In *Illuminations*, 83–102. New York: Schocken Books, 1978.

Black, Lydia. "The Russian Conquest of Kodiak." *Anthropological Papers of the University of Alaska* 24, 1–2 (1992): 165–82.

Blackman, Margaret. *During My Time: Florence Edenshaw Davidson, a Haida Woman.* Seattle: University of Washington Press, 1982.

Bodfish, Waldo. *Kusig: An Eskimo Life History from the Artic Coast of Alaska.* Recorded, compiled, and edited by William Schneider in collaboration with Leona Kisautaq and James Mumigana Nageak. Fairbanks: University of Alaska Press, 1991.

Bray, Tamara L., and Thomas W. Killian, eds. *Reckoning with the Dead.* Washington, D.C.: Smithsonian Institution Press, 1994.

Brettell, Caroline B., and Carolyn A. Sargent, eds. *Gender in Cross-Cultural Perspective.* 2d ed. Upper Saddle River, N.J.: Prentice Hall, 1997.

Brody, Hugh. *Maps and Dreams.* New York: Pantheon Books, 1981.

Bruner, Edward M., ed. *Text, Play, and Story.* Washington, D.C.: American Ethnological Society, 1984.

Chamberlain, J. Edward. "Telling Tales." *Connotations: The Journal of the Island Institute* 1, 1 (1993): 13–19.

Clifford, J. W., and George E. Marcus, eds. *Writing Culture: The Poetics and Politics of Ethnography.* Berkeley: University of California Press, 1986.

Crapanzano, Vincent. *Tuhami: Portrait of a Moroccan.* Chicago: University of Chicago Press, 1980.

Cruikshank, Julie. *Life Lived Like a Story.* Lincoln: University of Nebraska Press, 1991.

———. *The Social Life of Stories: Narrative and Knowledge in the Yukon Territory.* Lincoln: University of Nebraska Press, 1998.

Cruikshank, Moses. *The Life I've Been Living.* Recorded and edited by William Schneider. Fairbanks: University of Alaska Press, 1986.

Dauenhauer, Nora Marks, and Richard Dauenhauer, eds. *Haa Shuka'/*

*Our Ancestors: Tlingit Oral Narratives.* Vol. 1, *Classics of Tlingit Oral Literature.* Seattle: University of Washington Press, 1987.

Davis, Nancy Yaw. "Contemporary Pacific Eskimo." In *Handbook of North American Indians,* ed. D. Dumas, 198–204. Vol. 5. Washington, D.C.: Smithsonian Institution Press, 1984.

———. "Earthquake, Tsunami, Resettlement, and Survival in Two North Pacific Alaskan Native Villages." In *Natural Disasters and Cultural Responses,* ed. Anthony Oliver-Smith, 123–54. Studies in Third World Societies, no. 36. Williamsburg, Va.: Department of Anthropology, College of William and Mary, 1988.

———. *A Sociocultural Description of Small Communities in the Kodiak/Shumagin Region.* Prepared for Minerals Management Service, Alaska Outer Continental Shelf Region. Technical report, no. 121. Anchorage, Alaska: Cultural Dynamics, 1986.

———. "The *Exxon Valdez* Oil Spill, Alaska." In *The Long Road to Recovery: Community Responses to Industrial Disaster,* ed. James K. Mitchell, 231–72. New York: United Nations University Press, 1996.

Davis-Floyd, Robbie E. *Birth as an American Rite of Passage.* Berkeley: University of California, 1992.

Davydov, G. I. *Two Voyages to Russian America, 1802–1807.* Ed. Richard Pierce. Trans. Colin Bearne. Kingston, Canada: Limestone Press, 1977.

De Laurentis, Teresa. "The Essence of the Triangle or Taking the Risk of Essentialism Seriously: Feminist Theory in Italy, the U.S., and Britain." *Differences* 1, 2 (1989): 1–37.

Dixon, Mim. "The Changing Alaskan Experience: Health Care Services and Cultural Identity." *Western Journal of Medicine* 139, 6 (1983): 113–18.

Dixon, Mim, and Scott Kirchner. "Poking: An Eskimo Medical Practice in Northwest Alaska." *Etudes/Inuit/Studies* 6 (1982): 109–25.

Donta, Christopher. "Continuity and Function in the Ceremonial Material Culture of the Koniag Eskimo." In *Reckoning with the Dead,* ed.

Tamara L. Bray and Thomas W. Killian, 122–36. Washington, D.C.: Smithsonian Institution Press, 1994.

Douglas, Mary. *Purity and Danger: An Analysis of the Concepts of Pollution and Taboo*. London: Routledge and Kegan Paul, 1966.

Dwyer, Kevin. "The Dialogue of Ethnology." *Dialectical Anthropology* 4 (1979): 205–24.

Dye, Nancy Schrom. "The Medicalization of Birth." In *The American Way of Birth*, ed. P. S. Eakins, 21–46. Philadelphia: Temple University Press, 1986.

Fienup-Riordan, Ann. *Eskimo Essays*. New Brunswick, N.J.: Rutgers University Press, 1990.

———. "Following the Star: From the Ukraine to the Yukon." In *Russian America: The Forgotten Frontier*, ed. Barabara Sweetland Smith and Redmond J. Barnett. 227–36. Tacoma: Washington State Historical Society, 1990.

Fischer, Michael M. J. "Ethnicity and the Post-Modern Arts of Memory." In *Writing Culture: The Poetics and Politics of Ethnography*, ed. James Clifford and George E. Marcus, 194–233. Berkeley: University of California Press, 1986.

Fischer, Michael M. J., and George E. Marcus, eds. *Anthropology as Cultural Critique*. Chicago: University of Chicago Press, 1986.

Fishman, Joshua. *The Rise and Fall of the Ethnic Revival: Notes on Language and Ethnicity*. Berlin, Germany: Mouton, 1985.

Fitzhugh, William W., and Aron Crowell, eds. *Crossroads of Continents: Cultures of Siberia and Alaska*. Washington, D.C.: Smithsonian Institution Press, 1988.

Fortuine, Robert. "Health Care and the Alaska Native: Some Historical Perspectives." In *Polar Notes*, Occasional Publication of the Stafansson Collection, 1–42. Hanover, N.H.: Dartmouth College Library, 1975.

———. *Chills and Fever: Health and Disease in the Early History of Alaska*. Anchorage: University of Alaska Press, 1989.

Gluck, Sherna Berger, and Daphne Patai, eds. *Women's Words: The Feminist Practice of Oral History*. New York: Routledge, 1991.

Gmelch, Sharon. *Nan: The Life of an Irish Traveling Woman*. Prospect Heights, Ill.: Waveland Press, 1986.

Goody, Jack. *The Domestication of the Savage Mind*. London: Cambridge University Press, 1977.

Gottlieb, Alma, and Thomas Buckley, eds. *Blood Magic*. Berkeley: University of California Press, 1988.

Green, Rayna. *Native American Women: A Contextual Bibliography*. Bloomington: Indiana University Press, 1983.

Harding, Susan. "Women and Words in a Spanish Village." In *Toward an Anthropology of Women*, ed. Rayna R. Reiter, 283–308. New York: Monthly Review Press, 1975.

Holmberg, Heinrich Johan. *Holmberg's Ethnographic Sketches*. Ed. Marvin W. Falk. Trans. Fritz Jaensch. Rasmussen Library Historical Translation Series, no. 1. Fairbanks: University of Alaska Press, 1985.

Hrdlička, Aleš. *The Anthropology of Kodiak Island*. Philadelphia: Wistar Institute of Anatomy and Biology, 1944.

Hudson, Raymond L. "The Influence of Attu Weavers on Aleut Basketry." In *The Art of Native American Basketry*, ed. Frank W. Porter III, 335–43. Westport, Conn.: Greenwood Press, 1990.

Hymes, Dell. "Folklore's Nature and the Sun's Myth." *Journal of American Folklore* 88 (1975): 345–69.

———. *"In Vain I Tried to Tell You."* Philadelphia: University of Pennsylvania Press, 1981.

Jordan, Brigitte. *Birth in Four Cultures*. Montreal: Eden Press Women's Publications, 1980.

Jordan, Richard, and Richard A. Knecht. "Archaeological Research on Western Kodiak Island, Alaska: The Development of Koniag Culture." In *The Late Prehistoric Development of Alaska's Native People*, ed. Robert D. Shaw, Roger K. Hurritt, and Don E. Dumond, 356–453. Anchorage: Alaska Anthropological Association, 1988.

Jordan, Rosan A., and Susan J. Kalčik, eds. *Women's Folklore, Women's Culture*. Philadelphia: University of Pennsylvania Press, 1985.

Juul, Sandra. "Portrait of an Eskimo Tribal Doctor." *Alaska Medicine* 21 (November 1979): 66–71.

KANA KASITAQ: *Newsletter of the Kodiak Area Native Association*. Twentieth-anniversary edition, 1966–1986.

Katz, Richard. *Boiling Energy: Community Healing Among the Kalahari Kung*. Cambridge: Harvard University Press, 1982.

Katz, Richard, and Rachel Craig. "Community Healing: The Rich Resource of Tradition." *The Behavioral Sciences Exchange, College of Human and Rural Development Newsletter* 8, 2 (1987): 4–5.

Kawagley, Angayuqaq Oscar. *A Yupiaq World View: A Pathway to Ecology and Spirit*. Prospect Heights, Ill.: Waveland Press, 1995.

Kay, Margarita, ed. *The Anthropology of Human Birth*. Philadelphia: F. S. Davis, 1982.

Lakoff, George, and Mark Johnson. *Metaphors We Live By*. Chicago: University of Chicago Press, 1980.

Langness, L. L., and Gelya Frank. *Lives: An Anthropological Approach to Biography*. Novato, Calif.: Chandler and Sharp, 1981.

Linnekin, Jocelyn. "Defining Tradition: Variations on the Hawaiian Identity." *American Ethnologist* 10 (1983): 241–52.

Linton, Ralph. "Nativistic Movements." *American Anthropologist* 45, 2 (1943): 230–40.

Lisiansky, Urey. *A Voyage Round the World, 1803–1806*. London: John Booth and Longman, 1814.

Litoff, Judy Barrett. *American Midwives, 1860 to the Present*. Westport, Conn.: Greenwood Press, 1978.

Mason, Rachel. *Final Report: Community Preparation and Response to the Exxon Oil Spill in Kodiak, Alaska*. Boulder, Colo.: Quick Response Research, Natural Hazards Research and Applications Information Center, 1990.

———. "Fishing and Drinking in Kodiak, Alaska: The Sporadic Recreation of an Endangered Lifestyle." Ph.D. diss., University of Virginia, 1993.

―――. "The Alutiiq Ethnographic Bibliography." Kodiak, Alaska: Kodiak Area Native Association, 1995.

―――. "Russian Orthodox Church Readers in Kodiak Area Villages." Paper presented at the 1988 Kodiak Cultural Heritage Conference, Kodiak, Alaska, 1988.

McClain, Carol Shepherd, ed. *Women as Healers: Cross-Cultural Perspectives*. New Brunswick, N.J.: Rutgers University Press, 1989.

Mintz, Sidney. Foreword to *Afro-American Anthropology: Contemporary Perspectives*, ed. Norman E. Whitten Jr. and John F. Szwed, 1–16. New York: Free Press, 1970.

Mishler, Craig. "The Nuta'aq: Musical Folk Drama in English Bay." Paper presented at the annual meeting of the Alaska Anthropological Association, Fairbanks, Alaska, March 1988.

―――. "Aurcaq: Interruption, Distraction, and Reversal in an Alutiiq Men's Dart Game." *Journal of American Folklore* 110, 436 (1997): 189–202.

Morrow, Phyllis, and William Schneider, eds. *When Our Words Return: Writing, Hearing, and Remembering Oral Traditions of Alaska and the Yukon*. Logan: Utah State University Press, 1995.

Mulcahy, Joanne B. "How They Knew: Women's Talk about Healing on Kodiak Island, Alaska." In *Feminist Messages: Coding in Women's Folk Culture*, ed. Joan Newlon Radner, 183–202. Urbana: University of Illinois Press, 1993.

―――. "Through Dreams and Shadows." In *The Stories That Shape Us: Contemporary Women Write about the West*, ed. James Hepworth and Teresa Jordan, 243–61. New York: Norton, 1995.

Mulcahy, Joanne B., with Mary Peterson. "Mary Peterson: A Life of Healing and Renewal." In *Wings of Gauze: Women of Color and the Experience of Health and Illness*, ed. Barbara Bair and Susan E. Cayleff, 148–69. Detroit, Mich.: Wayne State University Press, 1993.

Napoleon, Harold. *Yuuyaraq: The Way of the Human Being*. Ed. Eric Madsen. Fairbanks: Center for Cross-Cultural Studies, University of Alaska, 1991.

Nice, Philip, with Walter Johnson, *The Alaska Health Aide Program: A Tradition of Helping Ourselves*. Anchorage, Alaska: Institute for Circumpolar Health Studies, 1998.

Oleksa, Father Michael. "Three Saints Bay and the Evolution of the Aleut Identity." Anchorage: Alaska Pacific University HCRS Village Histories Project, 1982.

——. "What Is the Proper Name for Kodiak Island Natives?" *Kodiak Times*, 17 October 1985, 4–6.

——. *Alaskan Mission Spirituality*. Mahwah, N.J.: Paulist Press, 1987.

——. "The Creoles and Their Contributions to the Development of Alaska." In *Russian America: The Forgotten Frontier*, ed. Barbara Sweetland Smith and Redmond J. Barnett, 185–95. Tacoma: Washington State Historical Society, 1990.

——. *Orthodox Alaska: A Theology of Mission*. Crestwood, N.Y.: St. Vladimir's Seminary Press, 1992.

Ong, Walter J. *Orality and Literacy*. New York: Methuen, 1982.

Parran, T., et al. *Alaska's Health: A Survey Report to the U.S. Department of the Interior*. Pittsburgh, Penn.: University of Pittsburgh Graduate School of Public Health, 1954.

Partnow, Patricia. "Ethnicity in the Twentieth Century: The Aluutiq Case." Paper presented at the Alaska Anthropological Meeting, Juneau, Alaska, March 1994.

Paulson, William R. *Enlightenment, Romanticism, and the Blind in France*. Princeton, N.J.: Princeton University Press, 1987.

Personal Narratives Group, eds. *Interpreting Women's Lives: Feminist Theory and Personal Narratives*. Bloomington: Indiana University Press, 1989.

Prucha, Francis P., ed. *The Dawes Act and the Allotment of Indian Lands*. Norman: University of Oklahoma Press, 1973.

Pullar, Gordon. "Proposal: A Gathering of the Alutiiq Nation." Unpublished manuscript, 1991.

———. "Ethnic Identity, Cultural Pride, and Generations of Baggage: A Personal Experience." *Arctic Anthropology* 29, 2 (1992): 182–91.

———. "Alutiiq." In *Native America in the Twentieth Century: An Encyclopedia*, ed. Mary B. Davis, 29–31. New York: Garland Publishing, 1994.

———. *Indigenous Culture and Organizational Culture: A Case Study of an Alaska Native Organization*. Ph.D. diss., Union Institute, 1997.

Radner, Joan Newlon, ed. *Feminist Messages: Coding in Women's Folk Culture*. Urbana: University of Illinois Press, 1993.

Robinson, Charles R. "Education in Alaska, 1884–1918." Master's thesis, University of Puget Sound, 1972.

Roppel, Patricia. *Alaska's Salmon Hatcheries, 1881–1959*. Anchorage: Alaska Historical Commission Studies in History, no. 20. 1982.

Rosaldo, Renato. "Doing Oral History." *Social Analysis* 4 (1980): 89–99.

Rostad, Michael. *A Time to Dance: Life of an Alaska Native*. Anchorage, Alaska: A. T. Publishing, 1988.

Samuel, Raphael, and Paul Thompson, eds. *The Myths We Live By*. New York: Routledge, 1990.

Schneider, William. "Lessons from Alaska Natives about Oral Tradition and Recordings." In *When Our Words Return: Writing, Hearing, and Remembering Oral Traditions of Alaska and the Yukon*, ed. Phyllis Morrow and William Schneider, 185–204. Logan: Utah State University Press, 1995.

Schrager, Samuel. "What Is Social in Oral History?" *International Journal of Oral History* 4 (1983): 72–98.

Shapsnikoff, Anefesia, and Raymond L. Hudson. "Aleut Basketry." *Anthropological Papers of the University of Alaska* 16, 2 (1974): 41–69.

Shostak, Marjorie. *Nisa: The Life and Words of a Kung Woman*. Cambridge: Harvard University Press, 1981.

Smith, Barbara Sweetland. *Preliminary Survey of Documents in the Archives of the Russian Orthodox Church in Alaska*. Boulder, Colo.: Western Interstate Commission for Higher Education, 1974.

———. "Russia's Cultural Legacy in America: The Orthodox Mission." In *Russian America: The Forgotten Frontier*, ed. Barbara Sweetland Smith and Redmond J. Barnett, 245–53. Tacoma: Washington State Historical Society, 1990.

Smith, Barbara Sweetland, and Redmond J. Barnett, eds. *Russian America: The Forgotten Frontier*. Tacoma: Washington State Historical Society, 1990.

Sollors, Werner. *Beyond Ethnicity: Consent and Descent in American Culture*. New York: Oxford University Press, 1986.

Stahl, Sandra K. D. "The Personal Narrative and Folklore." *Journal of the Folklore Institute* 14, 1–2 (1977): 9–30.

Susie, Debra Anne. *In the Way of Our Grandmothers: A Cultural View of Twentieth-Century Midwifery in Florida*. Athens: University of Georgia Press, 1988.

Tedlock, Dennis. *The Spoken Word and the Work of Interpretation*. Philadelphia: University of Pennsylvania Press, 1983.

Tikhmenev, Petr Alexandrovich. *A History of the Russian-American Company*. Vol. 2, *Documents*, ed. Richard A. Pierce and A. S. Donnelly. Kingston, Canada: Limestone Press, 1979.

Titon, Jeff Todd. "The Life Story." *Journal of American Folklore* 93, 369 (1980): 276–92.

Townsend, Joan. "Ranked Societies of the Alaska Pacific Rim." In *Alaska Native Culture and History*, ed. Yoshinobu Kotani and William B. Workman, 123–56. Senri Ethnological Series, no. 4. Osaka, Japan: National Museum of Ethnology, 1978.

Turner, Edith. *The Hands Feel It*. DeKalb: Northern Illinois University Press, 1996.

———. "Traditional Healing at Point Hope, Alaska." Unpublished manuscript.

Wallace, Anthony. "Revitalization Movements." *American Anthropologist* 58, 2 (1956): 264–81.

———. "Revitalization Processes." In *To See Ourselves: Anthropology and Modern Social Issues*, ed. Thomas Weaver, 470–74. Glenview, Ill.: Scott, Foresman, 1973.

Weaver, Howard, ed. "A People in Peril," *Anchorage Daily News*, 10–19 January 1988.

Weigle, Marta. *Spiders and Spinsters*. Albuquerque: University of New Mexico Press, 1992.

Williams, Walter L. *The Spirit and the Flesh*. Boston: Beacon Press, 1987.

# Index

Abu-Lughod, Lila, 137–38 (n. 16)
Afanasiia, ix
AFN, xii, 113
Agnot, Ephraim, 24, 131
Agnot, Irene, 50
Agnot, Miney, 14
Agnot, Simeon, 24
agudaq, 15
Aiaktalik, 75
Akhiok, xiii, xiv, 2–3, 130; alcoholism
    in, xx, 3, 78, 79, 80, 85, 87, 92, 97,
    98–99; author's visit to, 84–85,
    96, 101–2; cultural revitalization
    in, xx, 92–93, 96–99, 130; and
    the *Exxon Valdez* oil spill, 92, 97;
    foreign images of "the good life"
    in, 78, 146 (n. 1); health care in,
    31; school in, 31; social problems
    in, xx, 78; younger generation in,
    78, 79
Alaska Area Native Health Service,
    60
Alaska Federation of Natives (AFN),
    xii, 113

Alaska Humanities Forum, 1, 91
Alaska Maternal Child Health
    Coalition, 104, 132
Alaska Native Claims Settlement
    Act (ANCSA), xi , 62, 119, 144
    (n. 14)
Alaska Natives: and the American
    system, x–xi; conditions of, xii–xiii;
    terms for, 9, 10–11, 139–40
    (n. 6). *See also* Aleuts; Alutiiqs
Alaska Peninsula, 1, 10, 139–40
    (n. 6)
Alaska Rural Systemic Initiative, 116
Albert (grandson), 123
Alcoholics Anonymous (AA), 87, 93,
    98
alcoholism, xxi, 12, 129; in Akhiok,
    xx, 3, 78, 79, 80, 85, 87, 92, 97,
    98–99; factors contributing to,
    xxiii, 78–79, 93; as "infection of
    the soul," xxix; and Mary Peterson,
    xxvii, 80–82; programs to counter,
    87, 139 (n. 3)
Aleuts, 21, 129, 140 (n. 7); Mary

163

Brody, Hugh, 129
Bryn Mawr College, 86, 90, 91

*Call to Action, A* (AFN), xii–xiii
Cameron, Judy Eluska (daughter), 59, 86, 123
canneries, 34, 35, 36
Catherine the Great, xxi
cattle ranching, 138–39 (n. 2)
*Ceremony* (Silko), 132
Chamberlain, Ted, xxix
CHAs. *See* Community Health Aides
chemoaides, 61
Chichenoff, Katherine, xxiv
childbirth: as bio-social construct, 48; and CHAs, 62, 66; and cultural rebirth, xx; at home, xxiv, 12, 104; in hospitals, 46, 128; with midwives, xxv, xxix, 48; premature, 58–59; and risk, 63, 145 (n. 17); ritual preparation for, 44
CHPs (Community Health Practitioners), 62, 144–45 (n. 15)
Christening Day, 27
Christensen, Clyda, 38, 49, 57
Christensen, Sasha, 49
Christmas, 22–23, 24, 25, 98, 99
Chugachmiut, 104, 139–40 (n. 6)
Chya, Nida, 49
*ciqlluaq. See barabaras*
clothing, 17–18
Cohen, Rena, 68–69, 71, 120
colonization, x, xxi–xxii, xxix, 13, 135 (n. 1)
community: and the *Exxon Valdez* oil spill, 93; and healing, xxviii, 129;

Mary Peterson on, 126, 127; and women's resilience, xxx
Community Health Aide Program, 56, 60, 66
Community Health Aides (CHAs), xiii, 46, 133, 144 (n. 14), 144–45 (n. 15); and childbirth, 62–63, 66; and CHPs, 62; difficulty of role of, 62, 63, 66, 114; linked with midwives, xxv, 60–61, 62–63, 105, 107; and Mary Peterson, xx, xxvii, 60, 63, 64–65, 66–67, 95, 103–4, 114
Community Health Practitioners (CHPs), 62, 144–45 (n. 15)
Coyle, Irene, 127
Creoles, xxii, 10, 29, 135 (n. 3)
"Crossroads of Continents," 90
crowberries, 15, 115, 140 (n. 12)
Cruikshank, Julie, 132, 143 (n. 32), 147 (n. 14)
cultural revitalization: in Akhiok, 92–93, 96–97, 130; Alutiiq, 91, 134; and the Alutiiq Elders/Youth Conference, 119; and birth and rebirth, xx; and the elders, 116–17; on Kodiak Island, xxvi, 86, 90, 137 (nn. 8, 9); and Mary Peterson, xxvii; and midwives, 105; and Native healers, 133; and oral tradition, xxvii; signs of, 12; and terms for Native identity, 9

Dauenhauer, Nora, 96
Dauenhauer, Richard, 96
David (son), 92, 94, 97, 123

medicine, modern, xiii, xiv

Melcoulie, Katherine, 49

Melovedoff, Victor, 70

Melovedoff, Walter, 68

men, Native, 89

menstruation, 37–39, 143 (n. 32); Mary Peterson on, 39–40, 41, 57

Metlakatla, 30

Miatzic, 8

midwives and midwifery, xiv, xxiv–xxv; appointment of, 47; and "belonging," 125; and CHAs, xxv, 61, 62–63, 105, 107; compensation for work of, 111; and cultural renewal, 105; gathering of, 104, 112; and healing, xxiv, 50; and herbs, 45; "knowing" of, xix, xxiv, xxix, 44, 50, 105, 145 (n. 17); and Native identity, 50; postnatal care by, 110; power of, 58; prenatal care by, 44, 48, 110, 144 (n. 7); prior to Russian contact, 45; recalled by Mary Peterson, 56–57; stories about, xix, xxiv, 44, 48, 50, 56–57, 105–11, 128, 132–33; stories of blind, 49, 53, 57, 143 (n. 9); as symbol of cultural connection, 104; as symbol of resistance to outside influences, xxix; viewed by Kodiak Natives, xxiv–xxv; and Westerners, 47, 128

Mintz, Sidney, xxvi

Mishler, Craig, 23, 141 (n. 18), 141 (n. 19)

mission schools, 29, 142 (n. 24)

Mitchell (son), 94, 123, 130

mogolnik, 57

Momaday, N. Scott, 132, 134

Monroe, Mary, 91

Morgan, Thomas J., 30, 142 (n. 23)

Mulcahy, Joanne, xiv, xxii–xxiii, xxiv–xxvi, xxix–xxxi, 84; letters to Mary Peterson, 94–95, 111, 112–16

mumming, 23, 141 (n. 18)

myths: creation, 65, 145 (n. 18); about Oleanna, 70, 146 (n. 24); and women, 72

*Myths We Live By* (Thompson and Samuel), 72

Napoleon, Harold, xxviii–xxvix, 105

National Museum of Natural History, 134

Native Alaskans, 135–36 (n. 3)

Native Americans, 13

Nelson, Betty, 66, 121

Neseth, Eunice, 100, 147 (n. 13)

New Year's Eve, 23, 26–27, 99

Nick (son), 58

"Nuta'aq, The" (Mishler), 141 (n. 18)

Old Harbor, xxi, 14, 90, 139 (n. 3), 141 (n. 19)

Oleksa, Father Michael, 21, 79

Olga, ix

Ong, Walter, 107, 111, 147–48 (n. 15)

oral tradition, xxiv, xxvi, xxvii, 137 (n. 8)

Organic Act, 30

Orr, Dr., 11

Pacific Eskimo, 9, 10, 139–40 (n. 6)
pacifiers, 4, 121
Partnow, Patricia, 140 (n. 11)
"People in Peril, A," xii, 85
Pestriakov, Paraskeva, ix–x, xiv
Pestriakov, Sophiia, ix
Pestrikoff, Florence, 120
Pestrikoff, John, 124
Pestrikoff, Pariscovia, ix–x, xiv
Peterson, Frank, 3, 4, 125
Peterson, Joyce, 125
Peterson, Lawrence (brother), 94, 123, 131
Peterson, Mary: audience for stories of, 134; and the author, xxiii, xxv, xxx, 77, 84; on being Aleut, 127, 129; on "belonging," 125–26, 126–27; children of, 43, 58, 82, 86, 123, 126; early life of, 3–9; elder status held by, 118, 121–24; faith of, 21, 22, 23–29, 134; family names of, 2, 138 (n. 1); flight from Akhiok of, xx, xxiii, 77, 79, 81–82; healing knowledge of, xxvii; on the healing of Akhiok, 97–99; kinship network of, 94, 118, 123, 134; letters to author, 94–95, 111, 112–16; life history of, xxix–xxx, xxv–xxvi, xxxi; longing for village life, 79–80, 83–84; losses experienced by, 87–89, 127, 130–31; on marriage, 41–43; marriage of, 33, 41; on the old ways, 113–14; return to Akhiok, xx, 94, 96, 97, 102, 112; as role model, xx, xxvii; self-assurance and stature of, 121, 148 (n. 22); seventy-first birthday of, 1, 3, 121, 122; stories of being a midwife, xix, 50–56, 58, 63–64, 106–10, 111, 128; and the survival of Alutiiq people, xiv; traditional life of, xxvii

Peterson, Rena (Cohen), 120
Peterson, Senaphant (brother), 88
Peterson, Teacon (brothers), 6, 87
Peterson, Teacon (father), 3, 125
placenta, 110
plundering, xxxi, 138 (n. 17)
post-traumatic stress disorder, xxix, 93
pregnancy, 52–53
Prince William Sound, 1, 10, 91, 93, 139–40 (n. 6)
puberty seclusion, 37–39, 106, 143 (n. 32)
Pullar, Gordon L., 90, 118–19, 137 (n. 9), 139–40 (n. 6), 148 (n. 20); birth of, ix–x; and KANA, xi, xii, 86

Ralph (son), 58, 82, 104, 111
Randolph, Martha, 63
religion, 21–29, 48, 71
reservations, 30
Rogers, George, 89
Rostad, Michael, 142 (n. 26)
RuralCap, 93
Russian America, xxi, 135–36 (n. 3)
Russian-American Company, xxi
Russian Orthodoxy, 3, 11, 21, 24; and healing, xxv; and "knowing," xix–xx,